JAMESTOWN EDUCATION

W9-CGU-767

TIMED READINGS PLUS

25 Two-Part Lessons
with Questions for
Building Reading Speed and Comprehension

BOOK EIGHT

Edward Spargo

Glencoe McGraw-Hill

New York, New York   Columbus, Ohio   Chicago, Illinois

JAMESTOWN EDUCATION

Glencoe/McGraw-Hill

A Division of The McGraw·Hill Companies

Timed Readings Plus, Book Eight, Level K
Selection text adapted from Compton's Encyclopedia.
Used with permission of Compton's Learning Company.

ISBN: 0-89061-910-7

Send all inqueries to:
Glencoe/McGraw-Hill
130 E. Randolph Street
Suite 400
CHICAGO, Il. 60601

Printed in the United States of America
11 12 13 14   MAL 17 16 15 14

CONTENTS

TO THE INSTRUCTOR

Overview

Timed Readings Plus is designed to develop both reading speed and comprehension. A timed selection in each lesson focuses on improving reading rate. A nontimed selection—the "plus" selection—follows the timed selection. The nontimed selection concentrates on building mastery in critical areas of comprehension.

The 10 books in the series span reading levels 4–13, with one book at each level. Readability of the selections was assessed by using the Fry Readability Scale. Each book contains 25 lessons; each lesson is divided into Parts A and B.

Part A includes the timed selection followed by 10 multiple-choice questions: 5 fact questions and 5 thought questions. The timed selection is 400 words long and contains subject matter that is factual, nonfiction, and textbook-like. Because everyone—regardless of level—reads a 400-word passage, the steps for the timed selection can be concurrent for everyone.

Part B includes the nontimed selection, which is more narrative than the timed selection. The length of the selection varies depending on the subject matter, which relates to the content of the timed selection. The nontimed selection is followed by five comprehension questions that address the following major comprehension skills: recognizing words in context, distinguishing fact from opinion, keeping events in order, making correct inferences, and understanding main ideas.

Getting Started

Begin by assigning students to a level. A student should start with a book that is one level below his or her current reading level. If a student's reading level is not known, a suitable starting point would be one or two levels below the student's present grade in school.

Teaching a Lesson: Part A

Work in each lesson begins with the timed selection in Part A. If you wish to have all the students in the class read a selection at the same time, you can coordinate the timing using the following method. Give students the signal to preview. Allow 15 seconds for this. Have students begin reading the selection at the same time. After one minute has passed, write on the chalkboard the time that has elapsed. Update the time at 10-second intervals (1:00, 1:10, 1:20, etc.). Tell students to copy down the last time shown on the chalkboard when they finish reading. They should then record this reading time in the space designated after the selection.

If students keep track of their own reading times, have them write the times at which they start and finish reading on a separate piece of paper and then figure and record their reading time as above.

Students should now answer the ten questions that follow the Part A selection. Responses are recorded by putting an X in the box next to the student's choice of answer. Correct responses to eight or more questions indicates satisfactory comprehension and recall.

Teaching a Lesson: Part B

When students have finished Part A, they can move on to read the Part B selection. Although brief, these selections deliver all the content needed to attack the range of comprehension questions that follow.

Students next answer the comprehension questions that follow the Part B selection. Directions for answering the questions are provided with each question. Correct responses require deliberation and discrimination.

Correcting and Scoring Answers

Using the Answer Key at the back of the book, students self-score their responses to the questions in Parts A and B. Incorrect answers should be circled and the correct answers should be marked. The number of correct answers for Part A and for Part B and the total correct answers should be tallied on the final page of the lesson.

Using the Graphs

Reading times are plotted on the Reading Rate graph at the back of the book. The legend on the graph automatically converts reading times to words-per-minute rates. Comprehension totals are plotted on the Comprehension Scores graph. Plotting automatically converts the raw scores to a comprehension percentage based on four points per correct answer.

Diagnosis and Evaluation

The Comprehension Skills Profile graph at the back of the book tracks student responses to the Part B comprehension questions. For each incorrect response, students should mark an X in the corresponding box on the graph. A column of Xs rising above other columns indicates a specific comprehension weakness. Using the profile, you can assess trends in student performance and suggest remedial work if necessary.

A student who has reached a peak in reading speed (with satisfactory comprehension) is ready to advance to the next book in the series. Before moving on to the next book, students should be encouraged to maintain their speed and comprehension on a number of lessons in order to consolidate their achievement.

How to Use This Book

Getting Started

Study Part A: Reading Faster and Better. Read and learn the steps to follow and the techniques to use to help you read more quickly and more efficiently.

Study Part B: Mastering Reading Comprehension. Learn what the five categories of comprehension are all about. Knowing what kind of comprehension response is expected from you and how to achieve that response will help you better comprehend all you read.

Working a Lesson

Find the Starting Lesson. Locate the timed selection in Part A of the lesson that you are going to read. Wait for your instructor's signal to preview the selection. Your instructor will allow you 15 seconds for previewing.

Read the Part A Selection. When your instructor gives you the signal, begin reading. Read at a faster-than-normal speed. Read carefully so that you will be able to answer questions about what you have read.

Record Your Reading Time. When you finish reading, look at the blackboard and note your reading time. Write this time at the bottom of the page on the line labeled Reading Time.

Answer the Part A Questions. Answer the 10 questions that follow the selection. There are 5 fact questions and 5 thought questions. Choose the best answer to each question and put an X in that box.

Read the Part B Selection. This passage is less textbook-like and more story-like than the timed selection. Read well enough so that you can answer the questions that follow.

Answer the Part B Questions. These questions are different from traditional multiple-choice questions. In answering these questions, you must make three choices for each question. Instructions for answering each category of question are given. There are 15 responses for you to record.

Correct Your Answers. Use the Answer Key at the back of the book. For the Part A questions, circle any wrong answer and put an X in the box you should have marked. For the Part B questions, circle any wrong answer and write the correct letter or number next to it.

Scoring Your Work

Total Your Correct Answers. Count your correct answers for Part A and for Part B. Record those numbers on the appropriate lines at the end of the lesson. Then add the two scores to determine your total correct answers. Record that number on the appropriate line.

Plotting Your Progress

Plot Your Reading Time. Refer to the Reading Rate graph on page 116. On the vertical line that represents your lesson, put an X at the point where it intersects your reading time, shown along the left-hand side. The right-hand side of the graph will reveal your words-per-minute reading speed. Your instructor will review this graph from time to time to evaluate your progress.

Plot Your Comprehension Scores. Record your comprehension scores on the graph on page 117. On the vertical line that represents your lesson, put an X at the point where it intersects your total correct answers, shown along the left-hand side. The right-hand side of the graph will reveal your comprehension percentage. Your instructor will want to review this graph, too. Your achievement, as shown on both graphs, will determine your readiness to move on to higher and more challenging levels.

Plot Your Comprehension Skills. You will find the Comprehension Skills Profile on page 118. It is used to record your wrong answers only for the Part B questions. The five categories of questions are listed along the bottom. There are five columns of boxes, one column for each question. For every wrong answer, put an X in a box for that question. Your instructor will use this graph to detect any comprehension problems you may be experiencing.

PART A: READING FASTER AND BETTER

Step 1: Preview

When you read, do you start in with the first word, or do you look over the whole selection for a moment? Good readers preview the selection first. This helps make them good—and fast—readers. Here are the steps to follow when previewing the timed selection in Part A of each unit.

1. Read the Title. Titles are designed not only to announce the subject, but also to make the reader think. What can you learn from the title? What thoughts does it bring to mind? What do you already know about this subject?

2. Read the First Sentence. Read the first two sentences if they are short. The opening sentence is the writer's opportunity to greet the reader. Some writers announce what they hope to tell you in the selection. Some writers tell you why they are writing. Other writers just try to get your attention.

3. Read the Last Sentence. Read the final two sentences if they are short. The closing sentence is the writer's last chance to talk to you. Some writers repeat the main idea once more. Some writers draw a conclusion—this is what they have been leading up to. Other writers summarize their thoughts; they tie all the facts together.

4. Scan the Selection. Glance through the selection quickly to see what else you can pick up. Look for anything that can help you read the selection. Are there names, dates, or numbers? If so, you may have to read more slowly. Is the selection informative—containing a lot of facts, or is it conversational—an informal discussion with the reader?

Step 2: Read for Meaning

When you read, do you just see words? Are you so occupied reading words that you sometimes fail to get the meaning? Good readers see beyond the words—they seek the meaning. This makes them faster readers.

1. Build Concentration. You cannot read with understanding if you are not concentrating. When you discover that your thoughts are straying, correct the situation right away. Avoid distractions and distracting situations. Keep the preview information in mind. This will help focus your attention on the selection.

2. Read in Thought Groups. A reader should strive to see words in meaningful combinations. If you see only a word at a time (called word-by-word reading), your comprehension suffers along with your speed.

3. Question the Writer. To sustain the pace you have set for yourself, and to maintain a high level of concentration and comprehension, question the writer as you read. Ask yourself such questions as, "What does this mean? How can I use this information?"

Step 3: Grasp Paragraph Sense

The paragraph is the basic unit of meaning. If you can discover quickly and understand the main point of each paragraph, you can comprehend the writer's message. Good readers know how to find the main ideas quickly. This helps make them faster readers.

1. Find the Topic Sentence. The topic sentence, which contains the main idea, is often the first sentence of a paragraph. It is followed by sentences that support, develop, or explain the main idea. Sometimes a topic sentence comes at the end of a paragraph. When it does, the supporting details come first, building the base for the topic sentence. Some paragraphs do not have a topic sentence; all of the sentences combine to create a meaningful idea.

2. Understand Paragraph Structure. Every well-written paragraph has a purpose. The purpose may be to inform, define, explain, illustrate, and so on. The purpose should always relate to the main idea and expand on it. As you read each paragraph, see how the body of the paragraph is used to tell you more about the main idea.

Step 4: Organize Facts

When you read, do you tend to see a lot of facts without any apparent connection or relationship? Understanding how the facts all fit together to deliver the writer's message is, after all, the reason for reading. Good readers organize facts as they read. This helps them read rapidly and well.

1. Discover the Writer's Plan. Every writer has a plan or outline to follow. If you can discover the writer's method of organization, you have a key to understanding the message. Sometimes the writer gives you obvious signals. The statement, "There are three reasons . . .," should prompt you to look for a listing of the three items. Other less obvious signal words such as *moreover, otherwise,* and *consequently* tell you the direction the writer is taking in delivering a message.

2. Relate as You Read. As you read the selection, keep the information learned during the preview in mind. See how the writer is attempting to piece together a meaningful message. As you discover the relationship among the ideas, the message comes through quickly and clearly.

Part B: Mastering Reading Comprehension

Recognizing Words in Context

Always check to see if the words around a new word—its context—can give you some clue to its meaning. A word generally appears in a context related to its meaning. If the words *soil* and *seeds* appear in an article about gardens, for example, you can assume they are related to the topic of gardens.

Suppose you are unsure of the meaning of the word *expired* in the following paragraph:

> Vera wanted to take a book out, but her library card had expired.
> She had to borrow mine because she didn't have time to renew hers.

You could begin to figure out the meaning of *expired* by asking yourself, "What could have happened to Vera's library card that would make her have to borrow someone else's card?" You might realize that if she had to renew her card, it must have come to an end or run out. This would lead you to conclude that the word *expired* must mean to come to an end or run out. You would be right. The context suggested the meaning to you.

Context can also affect the meaning of a word you know. The word *key*, for instance, has many meanings. There are musical keys, door keys, and keys to solving a mystery. The context in which *key* occurs will tell you which meaning is right.

Sometimes a hard word will be explained by the words that immediately follow it. The word *grave* in the following sentence might give you trouble:

> He looked grave; there wasn't a trace of a smile on his lips.

You can figure out that the second part of the sentence explains the word *grave:* "wasn't a trace of a smile" indicates a serious look, so *grave* must mean serious.

The subject of a sentence and your knowledge about that subject might also help you determine the meaning of an unknown word. Try to decide the meaning of the word *revive* in the following sentence:

> Sunshine and water will revive those drooping plants.

The sentence is about giving plants light and water. You may know that plants need light and water to be healthy. If you know that drooping plants are not healthy, you can figure out that *revive* means to bring back to health.

Distinguishing Fact from Opinion

Every day you are called upon to sort out fact and opinion. When a friend says she saw Mel Gibson's greatest movie last night, she is giving you her opinion. When she says she saw Mel Gibson's latest movie, she may be stating a fact. The fact can be proved—you can check to confirm or verify that the movie is indeed Mel Gibson's most recent film. The opinion can be disputed—ask around and others may not agree about the film's unqualified greatness. Because much of what you read and hear contains both facts and opinions, you need to be able to tell them apart. You need the skill of distinguishing fact from opinion.

Facts are statements that can be proved true. The proof must be objective and verifiable. You must be able to check for yourself to confirm a fact.

Look at the following facts. Notice that they can be checked for accuracy and confirmed. Suggested sources for verification appear in parentheses.

- In 1998 Bill Clinton was president of the United States. (Consult newspapers, news broadcasts, election results, etc.)

- Earth revolves around the sun. (Look it up in encyclopedias or astrological journals; ask knowledgeable people.)

- Dogs walk on four legs. (See for yourself.)

Opinions are statements that cannot be proved true. There is no objective evidence you can consult to check the truthfulness of an opinion. Unlike facts, opinions express personal beliefs or judgments. Opinions reveal how someone feels about a subject, not the facts about that subject. You might agree or disagree with someone's opinion, but you cannot prove it right or wrong.

Look at the following opinions. Reasons for classification as opinions appear in parentheses.

- Bill Clinton was born to be a president. (You cannot prove this by referring to birth records. There is no evidence to support this belief.)

- Intelligent life exists on other planets in our solar system. (There is no proof of this. It may be proved true some day, but for now it is just an educated guess—not a fact.)

- Dog is man's best friend. (This is not a fact; your best friend might not be a dog.)

As you read, be aware that facts and opinions are frequently mixed together. The following passage contains both facts and opinions:

> The new 2000 Cruising Yacht offers lots of real-life interior room. It
> features a luxurious aft cabin, not some dim "cave." The galley

comes equipped with a full-size refrigerator and freezer. And this spacious galley has room to spare. The heads (there are two) have separate showers. The fit and finish are beyond equal and the performance is responsive and outstanding.

Did you detect that the third and fifth sentences state facts and that the rest of the sentences express opinions? Both facts and opinions are useful to you as a reader. But to evaluate what you read and to read intelligently, you need to know the difference between them.

Keeping Events in Order

Writers organize details in a pattern. They present information in a certain order. Recognizing how writers organize—and understanding that organization—can help you improve your comprehension.

When details are arranged in the precise order in which they occurred, a writer is using a chronological (or time) pattern. A writer may, however, change this order. The story may "flash back" to past events that affected the present. The story may "flash forward" to show the results of present events. The writer may move back and forth between past, present, and future to help you see the importance of events.

Making Correct Inferences

Much of what you read suggests more than it says. Writers do not always state outright what they want you to know. Frequently, they omit information that underlies the statements they make. They may assume that you already know it. They may want you to make the effort to figure out the implied information. To get the most out of what you read, you must come to an understanding about unstated information. You can do this through inference. From what is stated, you make inferences about what is not.

You make many inferences every day. Imagine, for example, that you are visiting a friend's house for the first time. You see a bag of dog food. You infer (make an inference) that the family has a dog. On another day you overhear a conversation. You catch the names of two actors and the words *scene, dialogue,* and *directing.* You infer that the people are discussing a movie or play.

In these situations and others like them, you infer unstated information from what you observe or read. Readers who cannot make inferences cannot see beyond the obvious. For the careful reader, facts are just the beginning. Facts stimulate your mind to think beyond them—to make an inference about what is meant but not stated.

The following passage is about Charles Dickens. As you read it, see how many inferences you can make.

Charles Dickens visited the United States in 1867. Wherever he went, the reception was the same. The night before, crowds arrived and lined up before the door. By morning the streets were campgrounds, with men, women, and children sitting or sleeping on blankets. Hustlers got ten times the price of a ticket. Once inside, audiences were surprised to hear their favorite Dickens characters speak with an English accent. After 76 readings Dickens boarded a ship for England. When his fellow passengers asked him to read, he said he'd rather be put in irons!

Did you notice that many inferences may be drawn from the passage? Dickens attracted huge crowds. From that fact you can infer that he was popular. His English accent surprised audiences. You can infer that many people didn't know he was English. Hustlers got high prices for tickets. This suggests that "scalping" tickets is not new. Dickens refused to read on the ship. You can infer that he was exhausted and tired of reading aloud to audiences. Those are some obvious inferences that can be made from the passage. More subtle ones can also be made; however, if you see the obvious ones, you understand how inferences are made.

Be careful about the inferences you make. One set of facts may suggest several inferences. Not all of them will be correct; some will be faulty inferences. The correct inference is supported by enough evidence to make it more likely than other inferences.

Understanding Main Ideas

The main idea tells who or what is the subject of the paragraph or passage. The main idea is the most important idea, the idea that provides purpose and direction. The rest of the paragraph or passage explains, develops, or supports the main idea. Without a main idea, there would be only a collection of unconnected thoughts. It would be like a handle and a bowl without the "idea cup," or bread and meat without the "idea sandwich."

In the following passage, the main idea is printed in italics. As you read, observe how the other sentences develop or explain the main idea.

Typhoon Chris hit with full fury today on the central coast of Japan. Heavy rain from the storm flooded the area. High waves carried many homes into the sea. People now fear that the heavy rains will cause mudslides in the central part of the country. The number of people killed by the storm may climb past the 200 mark by Saturday.

In this paragraph, the main idea statement appears first. It is followed by sentences that explain, support, or give details. Sometimes the main idea appears at the end of a paragraph. Writers often construct that type of paragraph when their purpose is to persuade or convince. Readers may be more open to a new idea if the reasons for it are presented first. As you read the following paragraph, think about the overall impact of the supporting ideas. Their purpose is to convince the reader that the main idea in the last sentence should be accepted.

> Last week there was a head-on collision at Huntington and Canton streets. Just a month ago a pedestrian was struck there. Fortunately, she was only slightly injured. In the past year there have been more accidents there than at any other corner in the city. In fact, nearly 10 percent of all city accidents occur there. This intersection is dangerous, and a traffic signal should be installed there before a life is lost.

The details in the paragraph progress from least important to most important. They achieve their full effect in the main idea statement at the end.

In many cases, the main idea is not expressed in a single sentence. The reader is called upon to interpret all of the ideas expressed and decide upon a main idea. Read the following paragraph:

> The American author Jack London was once a pupil at the Cole Grammar School in Oakland, California. Each morning the class sang a song. When the teacher noticed that Jack wouldn't sing, she sent him to the principal. He returned to class with a note. It said that he could be excused from singing if he would write an essay every morning.

In this paragraph, the reader has to interpret the individual ideas and decide on a main idea. This main idea seems reasonable: Jack London's career as a writer began with a "punishment" in grammar school.

Understanding the concept of the main idea and knowing how to find it is important. Transferring that understanding to your reading and study is also important.

1 A Seeker of Gold

Spanish explorer Hernando de Soto was one of the best-known gold seekers in history. Born in about 1500 in Barcarroto, Spain, de Soto came to the Americas when he was in his teens. He soon became a ruthless soldier whose troops feared his temper but admired his horse riding ability. In the 1520s, de Soto took part in expeditions to Central America, and in 1532, he helped Francisco Pizarro conquer Peru. By the time he returned to Spain, de Soto had great wealth gained from his share of treasures stolen from the Peruvians. But he was not yet satisfied; he had listened to the tales of American Indians and wanted to find the land of riches they described.

Captive American Indians had told the Spanish of lands north of Florida that had great riches—riches far greater than those of Mexico and Peru. De Soto hoped to win another fortune by finding these riches. He persuaded the Spanish king to appoint him governor of Cuba and Florida and to allow him to lead an expedition to explore North America. De Soto recruited hundreds of soldiers, and he and this great army set sail from Spain in April 1538. At Havana, Cuba, they set up an advance base and made final preparations for their expedition.

On May 30, 1539, de Soto and his army arrived in Florida, and from there, they marched northward to Georgia. They then changed directions and followed the Alabama River to Mobile Bay.

During the expedition, de Soto and his troops met many Indians whom they forced to furnish supplies and whose chiefs they tortured in a useless effort to locate the hidden gold. This brutality resulted in many battles; the bloodiest was fought near Mobile Bay. About 70 Spaniards were killed, and many more were wounded, including de Soto.

In the spring of 1541 as they continued their vain search for gold, de Soto and his army first saw the Mississippi River near the present site of Memphis, Tennessee. Building boats, they crossed the Mississippi and, by the next autumn, reached the Neosho River in northeastern Oklahoma.

In the spring of 1542, de Soto led his worn and tattered troops southward, and near the junction of the Red and the Mississippi Rivers, fell ill and died. Although his troops continued on to Mexico, they never found the great wealth the American Indians kept saying was just ahead.

Reading Time _____

Recalling Facts

1. Hernando de Soto was born in about 1500 in
   - ❏ a. Spain.
   - ❏ b. North America.
   - ❏ c. Peru.

2. De Soto helped Francisco Pizarro conquer
   - ❏ a. Peru.
   - ❏ b. Cuba.
   - ❏ c. Florida.

3. De Soto and his troops explored the country north of Florida in order to
   - ❏ a. conquer American Indians.
   - ❏ b. find reported riches.
   - ❏ c. establish a Spanish base in North America.

4. De Soto crossed the Mississippi River
   - ❏ a. by wading across.
   - ❏ b. in boats his troops built.
   - ❏ c. in Indian canoes.

5. De Soto died
   - ❏ a. before finding gold.
   - ❏ b. in an Indian battle.
   - ❏ c. after returning to Spain.

Understanding Ideas

6. A word that best describes de Soto is
   - ❏ a. kindly.
   - ❏ b. greedy.
   - ❏ c. brave.

7. You can conclude from the article that at the time of de Soto's expedition, North America was inhabited mostly by
   - ❏ a. Spanish explorers.
   - ❏ b. European settlers.
   - ❏ c. American Indians.

8. The article suggests that Spanish explorers in North America were motivated by
   - ❏ a. the thrill of discovering new lands.
   - ❏ b. the lure of riches.
   - ❏ c. a desire to meet new and different people.

9. The article suggests that de Soto's troops explored
   - ❏ a. most of North America.
   - ❏ b. northwestern North America.
   - ❏ c. southeastern North America.

10. It is likely that Indians reported gold to de Soto
    - ❏ a. even though they had no knowledge of it.
    - ❏ b. because they wanted a share of the riches.
    - ❏ c. to reward him for his kindness.

No Cure

"We Spaniards," said the conquistador Hernán Cortés, "suffer from a disease that only gold can cure." To seek relief from this disease, Spaniards like Hernando de Soto turned from the conquest of Mexico and Peru to the lands farther north. Lured on by stories of "El Dorado"—a city of gold—the conquistadors went from village to village, never finding the great wealth they sought.

Over a period of four years, Hernando de Soto crossed much of the present-day southeastern United States, vainly searching for El Dorado. Although supplies grew short and his troops were ragged and weary, de Soto refused to give up his search for wealth. When news came that supply ships were waiting on the Gulf of Mexico to carry him and his troops to safety, de Soto kept it to himself because he was afraid that the troops would rebel. He pushed them on, still looking for gold, and then in May 1542, de Soto fell ill with a fever and died.

Luis de Moscoso de Alvarado took over the expedition and led the survivors west, reaching what is now Texas. Short of supplies, they backtracked toward the Mississippi River where they built boats to carry them south. After four years of Spanish terror, however, the native population had had enough. As the Spaniards floated down the river in 1543, they were attacked by warriors in canoes. Finally, the few who remained reached Mexico.

1. Recognizing Words in Context

Find the word *pushed* in the passage. One definition below is a *synonym* for that word; it means the same or almost the same thing. One definition is an *antonym;* it has the opposite or nearly opposite meaning. The other has a completely different meaning. Label the definitions S for *synonym*, A for *antonym*, and D for *different*.

_____ a. shoved

_____ b. forced

_____ c. restrained

2. Distinguishing Fact from Opinion

Two of the statements below present *facts,* which can be proved correct. The other statement is an *opinion,* which expresses someone's thoughts or beliefs. Label the statements F for *fact* and O for *opinion.*

_____ a. De Soto never found the wealth he sought.

_____ b. All Spaniards suffered from a disease that only gold could cure.

_____ c. De Soto kept the news of the ships from his troops.

3. Keeping Events in Order

Label the statements below 1, 2, and 3 to show the order in which the events happened.

_____ a. De Soto did not let his troops know about ships that could take them to safety.

_____ b. The survivors built boats to carry them south.

_____ c. Warriors in canoes attacked the Spaniards.

4. Making Correct Inferences

Two of the statements below are correct *inferences*, or reasonable guesses. They are based on information in the passage. The other statement is an incorrect, or faulty, inference. Label the statements C for *correct* inference and F for *faulty* inference.

_____ a. De Soto was more concerned with finding gold than with his troops' safety.

_____ b. The American Indians of the Southeast did not have great riches.

_____ c. De Soto would have been satisfied if he had found even a little gold.

5. Understanding Main Ideas

One of the statements below expresses the main idea of the passage. One statement is too general, or too broad. The other explains only part of the passage; it is too narrow. Label the statements M for *main idea*, B for *too broad*, and N for *too narrow*.

_____ a. Hernando de Soto died of a fever in 1542.

_____ b. During the 1500s, Spanish expeditions explored the southern part of what is now the United States.

_____ c. The expedition led by Hernando de Soto in the southeastern part of what is now the United States was a failure.

Correct Answers, Part A _____

Correct Answers, Part B _____

Total Correct Answers _____

16

The Robin: Songster or Pest?

One of the best-known American birds is the robin, a member of the thrush family. Male robins are about ten inches (25 centimeters) long and have black heads, dark-gray upper parts, red breasts, yellow bills, and tails tipped with white at the outer corners. Females and young males are paler.

Nesting throughout North America from northern Alaska and Canada to southern Mexico, the robin is considered by many northerners as an early sign of spring. People in the north welcome the robin's musical warble, "cheerily, cheer up, cheerily," as an announcement that the long days of winter are drawing to an end.

After a sunrise concert, a robin begins its search for food by checking lawns for worms. It stands still, with its black head cocked to one side, and then suddenly darts at the ground, tugs violently, and pulls out a worm. In its search, a robin tilts its head back and forth rapidly and frequently. People once thought that the bird turned its head to listen to the ground for movement, but actually, the rapid head turning helps the robin better see nearby movement. In addition to worms, a robin also eats large quantities of insects. However, more than 50 percent of its diet consists of fruits and berries.

Robins build their cup-shaped nests on the horizontal branches of trees, in vines, and in eaves. The nest is made of mud, reinforced with coarse grass, leaves, and roots and lined with grass. A robin lays from four to six greenish-blue eggs two to three times a season. After the eggs hatch, both parents provide care until the hatchlings leave the nest in about 15 days; then the male robin takes over all care-giving chores as the mother prepares for the next brood.

After the nesting season is over, robins gather in flocks, roam about in search of food, and start their migration south. A few hardy individuals may winter in the north, taking refuge against storm and cold in deep evergreens and wooded swamps, but most wing their way south for the winter. The southern states know robins chiefly as winter residents whose cheery song is seldom appreciated and whose feeding habits greatly damage fruit and berry crops. While the robin is the state bird of the northern states of Michigan, Wisconsin, and Connecticut, it is not so honored in the southern states where many consider it a destructive pest.

Reading Time _____

Recalling Facts

1. The robin's diet consists mostly of
   - ❏ a. insects.
   - ❏ b. fruits and berries.
   - ❏ c. worms.

2. The robin's nest is made out of reinforced
   - ❏ a. twigs.
   - ❏ b. mud.
   - ❏ c. grass.

3. Robins lay eggs
   - ❏ a. once a season.
   - ❏ b. two or three times a season.
   - ❏ c. six times a year.

4. In the south, robins are chiefly
   - ❏ a. summer residents.
   - ❏ b. spring residents.
   - ❏ c. winter residents.

5. The male robin is the sole caregiver of
   - ❏ a. the eggs before they hatch.
   - ❏ b. hatchlings in the nest.
   - ❏ c. the young after they leave the nest.

Understanding Ideas

6. A robin is more likely to be appreciated by a person living in
   - ❏ a. Illinois.
   - ❏ b. Georgia.
   - ❏ c. Florida.

7. The robin is the state bird of Michigan, Wisconsin, and Connecticut, which suggests that
   - ❏ a. there are many robins in each of those states.
   - ❏ b. robins live in only those states.
   - ❏ c. robins prefer cold weather.

8. It is likely that female robins are paler than adult males because
   - ❏ a. females are shyer.
   - ❏ b. males like to show off.
   - ❏ c. then they are less visible while nesting.

9. A strawberry farmer is likely to consider robins
   - ❏ a. a welcome sign of spring.
   - ❏ b. cheerful songbirds.
   - ❏ c. destructive pests.

10. The robin is easily recognized probably because of its
    - ❏ a. white-tipped tail.
    - ❏ b. red breast.
    - ❏ c. yellow beak.

A Symbol of Spring and Summer

Toward the end of February, people in the northern states start asking, "Have you seen a robin?" By the second week of March, reports of robin sightings begin even though snow may still be in the forecast.

By April, robins begin their nesting ritual, as the male sings to mark territory and to chase off other birds, and the female makes a nest and lays the eggs. The parents take turns roosting, and in about two weeks, they welcome a new brood of featherless babies with huge, brightly colored mouths. The parents respond to the open mouths and fluttering wings by foraging tirelessly for food to feed their hungry youngsters.

When the babies are old enough to fly, they sit on the edge of the nest and flap their wings, sometimes tumbling out. Their parents then hurry to their defense, diving and pecking at any person or animal whose approach threatens the fallen flyers in training. Chirping encouragement, the parents urge the youngsters to seek shelter.

As food supplies dwindle in the fall, robins begin to gather in large groups in anticipation of the migration south, but they are casual about it. When food supplies are readily available, individual robins may often delay their migration or remain north throughout the winter.

1. Recognizing Words in Context

Find the word *foraging* in the passage. One definition below is a *synonym* for that word; it means the same or almost the same thing. One definition is an *antonym*; it has the opposite or nearly opposite meaning. The other has a completely different meaning. Label the definitions S for *synonym*, A for *antonym*, and D for *different*.

_____ a. waiting

_____ b. searching

_____ c. hoping

2. Distinguishing Fact from Opinion

Two of the statements below present *facts*, which can be proved correct. The other statement is an *opinion*, which expresses someone's thoughts or beliefs. Label the statements F for *fact* and O for *opinion*.

_____ a. Robin eggs hatch in about two weeks.

_____ b. Both parents sit on the nest.

_____ c. Robins are casual about flying south.

3. Keeping Events in Order

Label the statements below 1, 2, and 3 to show the order in which the events happened.

_____ a. The female robin builds a nest.

_____ b. Both parents feed the babies.

_____ c. Robins arrive in the northern states.

4. Making Correct Inferences

Two of the statements below are correct *inferences*, or reasonable guesses. They are based on information in the passage. The other statement is an incorrect, or faulty, inference. Label the statements C for *correct* inference and F for *faulty* inference.

_____ a. People in the north eagerly await the robins' arrival.

_____ b. Robins do not appear at any particular time.

_____ c. Robins are generally good parents.

5. Understanding Main Ideas

One of the statements below expresses the main idea of the passage. One statement is too general, or too broad. The other explains only part of the passage; it is too narrow. Label the statements M for *main idea*, B for *too broad*, and N for *too narrow*.

_____ a. Robins are popular in the northern states.

_____ b. The male robin sings while the female builds the nest.

_____ c. During the summer and spring in the northern states, robins breed and raise their young and then they usually fly south for the winter.

Correct Answers, Part A _____

Correct Answers, Part B _____

Total Correct Answers _____

Hunting began as a means of supplying food. In the Americas, native peoples obtained much of their food by killing buffalo, bear, deer, and waterfowl; and they used skins for clothing and shelter and bones for tools. Early European settlers also depended largely upon wildlife for meat.

Later, as farming and stock raising spread and many societies became more industrialized, hunting ceased to be a significant means of livelihood. Now hunting is primarily a sport that involves the seeking, pursuing, and killing of wild animals, called game, and birds, called game birds. Today, firearms are usually the hunting weapon of choice although some hunters use bow and arrows.

Critics of game hunting call it a blood sport that causes suffering and death to inoffensive animals, and they note that most people do not need to hunt to survive. Critics also point out that the tons of lead from shotgun cartridges and bullets left in the environment each year have effected a steady increase in toxic lead poisoning in animals, including endangered species, that ingest it. Proponents of game hunting point out that killing animals quickly is often more humane than letting them gradually starve in overpopulated regions with limited food supplies.

Through the years, the steady increase in the number of licensed hunters had at times threatened to wipe out the game supply. Since the late 1930s, however, reasonable conservation practices have been keeping the population of many species at an elevated level despite increased hunting pressures. Hunters should emulate the principle that guided American Indians: Kill only the game you want for food; never waste it.

The four major types of hunting game in the United States are upland game, waterfowl, big game, and pest. Upland game includes rabbits, squirrels, quail, pheasants, grouse, and woodcock. Geese and ducks are the favorite waterfowl targets. Big-game hunters stalk deer, bear, elk, antelope, and moose. Pest hunting may target coyotes in the West, crows on the farm, or woodchucks (groundhogs) almost everywhere.

Much of the enjoyment of hunting comes from just being in the fields or lowlands enjoying nature. Many hunters add to their pleasure by using a hunting dog. Dogs were probably trained to hunt as early as Neolithic times and came to be bred for their specialized skills. A well-trained dog can find game that would escape a hunter's eye, and some dogs make excellent retrievers of downed game.

Reading Time _____

Recalling Facts

1. Originally, game hunting was
   - ❏ a. a sport.
   - ❏ b. a means of supplying food.
   - ❏ c. a means of supplying domestic animals.

2. Today people hunt mainly for
   - ❏ a. sport.
   - ❏ b. food needed to survive.
   - ❏ c. pest control.

3. Big-game hunters stalk such animals as
   - ❏ a. rabbits and coyotes.
   - ❏ b. squirrels and geese.
   - ❏ c. elk and bear.

4. Today, the preferred hunting weapons are
   - ❏ a. bow and arrows.
   - ❏ b. dogs.
   - ❏ c. firearms.

5. In the West, coyotes are considered
   - ❏ a. animal pests.
   - ❏ b. big-game animals.
   - ❏ c. upland-game animals.

Understanding Ideas

6. The difference between early hunting and hunting today is that
   - ❏ a. hunting today is not a means of survival.
   - ❏ b. early hunters did not enjoy the sport.
   - ❏ c. today there are fewer animals to hunt.

7. You can conclude from the article that conservation efforts today are necessary because
   - ❏ a. critics of game hunting threatened to strike.
   - ❏ b. animals are not producing young in sufficient numbers.
   - ❏ c. hunters killed more animals than they could use for food.

8. It is likely that the invention of firearms
   - ❏ a. made it easier for hunters to kill their prey.
   - ❏ b. hindered hunters more than helped them.
   - ❏ c. made no difference in hunting.

9. You can conclude that hunting
   - ❏ a. should be outlawed.
   - ❏ b. has both positive and negative aspects.
   - ❏ c. is the best way to control animal populations.

10. You can conclude that hunters and critics of hunting
    - ❏ a. will always be in conflict.
    - ❏ b. have basically the same outlook regarding killing animals.
    - ❏ c. will agree on the best way to hunt.

The Buffalo Hunt

The scouts returned to camp with news of a nearby herd of buffalo. The chief told the women to get their travois—carriers formed by two poles in a *V*-shape with a hide lashed between them and pulled by a dog. The men and women went out together, approaching the herd from downwind so that the buffalo could not smell them.

The women set their travois upright in the ground, spaced like fence posts. They tied the poles together and then hid behind this barricade with the dogs. Meanwhile, two men had gone upwind of the herd, and charging the buffalo, they stampeded the herd toward the fence. Other men closed in from the sides, forcing the buffalo together, the women began shouting, and the dogs barked loudly. All the commotion confused the buffalo, which began to mill around in a tight group.

Now the men rushed in, shooting arrows and plunging lances into the herd animals. After the kill, the chief counted the dead buffalo and divided the meat equally among all the families. Two young men brought choice pieces of meat to the medicine man. Although the medicine man had not joined the hunt, his power had made it successful, and so he too received a share of the meat.

1. **Recognizing Words in Context**

   Find the word *mill* in the passage. One definition below is a *synonym* for that word; it means the same or almost the same thing. One definition is an *antonym;* it has the opposite or nearly opposite meaning. The other has a completely different meaning. Label the definitions S for *synonym,* A for *antonym,* and D for *different.*

   _____ a. circle

   _____ b. rest

   _____ c. grind

2. **Distinguishing Fact from Opinion**

   Two of the statements below present *facts,* which can be proved correct. The other statement is an *opinion,* which expresses someone's thoughts or beliefs. Label the statements F for *fact* and O for *opinion.*

   _____ a. Two men drove the herd toward the fence.

   _____ b. Behind the fence, the women shouted and the dogs barked.

   _____ c. This method was a clever way to hunt buffalo.

3. Keeping Events in Order

Two of the statements below describe events that happened at the same time. The other statement describes an event that happened before or after those events. Label them S for *same time*, B for *before*, and A for *after*.

_____ a. The women built a barricade with their travois and hid behind it.

_____ b. Two men went upwind of the herd.

_____ c. Other men closed in on the herd from the sides.

4. Making Correct Inferences

Two of the statements below are correct *inferences*, or reasonable guesses. They are based on information in the passage. The other statement is an incorrect, or faulty, inference. Label the statements C for *correct* inference and F for *faulty* inference.

_____ a. The buffalo hunters killed only as many buffalo as they needed.

_____ b. The buffalo hunters did not have horses.

_____ c. Buffalo are easily confused and frightened.

5. Understanding Main Ideas

One of the statements below expresses the main idea of the passage. One statement is too general, or too broad. The other explains only part of the passage; it is too narrow. Label the statements M for *main idea*, B for *too broad*, and N for *too narrow*.

_____ a. A band of buffalo hunters cooperated in a successful hunt.

_____ b. The hunters approached the buffalo from downwind so that the animals could not smell them.

_____ c. The life of the American Indians on the Plains centered on buffalo hunting.

Correct Answers, Part A _____

Correct Answers, Part B _____

Total Correct Answers _____

Clothing Through the Ages

No one knows for sure when clothing was first used, but it probably appeared between 25,000 and 50,000 years ago. It is believed that Neanderthals, who lived in caves in central Europe, wrapped themselves in animal furs, which may have been the first clothing. It is likely that the Neanderthal people noticed that fur-bearing animals were not bothered by the cold and so they began to use animal skins to cover themselves. These early garments had no sleeves or fastenings, rather they were simply wrapped around the body like a large cape. Later, people learned to cut and lace the skins so that they fitted the body more closely.

Much later, in about 7000 or 6000 B.C., people began to raise animals and cultivate crops, and gradually they learned to twist the wool from sheep and fibers from the flax plant into yarn. They then used primitive looms to weave the yarn into rectangles of cloth, which they draped around their bodies and fastened with a tie around their waists. This kind of draped garment was worn by the early Egyptians.

Such garments were also worn by the ancient Greeks and Romans, who gracefully draped fabric over their bodies. They often used fabrics with painted or embroidered decorative borders.

In about 1500 B.C., people of China learned to cultivate the silkworm and to weave its fragile filaments into very delicate fabric. The Chinese fashioned the fine silk cloth into flowing garments with long, loose sleeves.

The Japanese of the third century B.C. developed the technique of weaving a design into cloth. They made exquisite cloths by weaving colored and metallic threads in the patterns of flowers and birds. Such luxurious fabrics, called damasks or brocades, are still used in fine clothing.

During the Middle Ages, the art of weaving was so well developed that artisans were able to create woven picture hangings called tapestries. During this period, both men and women wore garments made from velvets or brocades.

Between the Middle Ages and the Industrial Revolution, there were few improvements in the methods of making cloth and clothing, and most people still made clothing at home. The Industrial Revolution with the invention of the spinning jenny, looms, and sewing machine helped change where and how clothing was produced. Before long, most clothing was made in factories. Today, factories use natural and synthetic fibers to produce a wide range of clothing styles.

Reading Time _____

Recalling Facts

1. The first clothing was
   - ❏ a. silk.
   - ❏ b. cloth made from animal hair.
   - ❏ c. animal skins.

2. Early Egyptians wore clothing made from
   - ❏ a. silk.
   - ❏ b. wool and flax yarns.
   - ❏ c. brocades.

3. The technique of weaving a design into cloth was developed by the people of
   - ❏ a. Japan.
   - ❏ b. Greece.
   - ❏ c. Rome.

4. Garments made from velvets or brocades were popular during the
   - ❏ a. Roman Empire.
   - ❏ b. Middle Ages.
   - ❏ c. Industrial Revolution.

5. Woven picture hangings are called
   - ❏ a. tapestries.
   - ❏ b. damasks.
   - ❏ c. brocades.

Understanding Ideas

6. You can conclude from the article that people first wore clothing
   - ❏ a. for decoration.
   - ❏ b. to keep warm.
   - ❏ c. to look like animals.

7. You can conclude that the clothing of the ancient Romans was most like that of the
   - ❏ a. Neanderthals.
   - ❏ b. Chinese.
   - ❏ c. Egyptians.

8. You can conclude that clothes made before the Industrial Revolution were
   - ❏ a. machine sewn.
   - ❏ b. hand sewn.
   - ❏ c. sewn without decoration.

9. Probably the most important influence on early clothing was
   - ❏ a. the silkworm.
   - ❏ b. weaving.
   - ❏ c. knitting.

10. You can conclude that clothing
    - ❏ a. has changed very little over the centuries.
    - ❏ b. will become less important in the future.
    - ❏ c. has changed a great deal over the centuries.

4   B   From Function to Fashion

In ancient times, clothing was generally not fitted to the body. People wore whole animal skins, and clothes made from woven material usually consisted of rectangular pieces of cloth draped in some way and secured by a tie.

In early Europe, people grew flax or raised sheep for wool. They spun their own thread from the flax and wool and wove it into cloth. They then fashioned the uncut cloth into tunics, sometimes stitched up the sides or down the middle, that they tied with rope. They used clothing mainly for warmth and protection, not as a fashion statement.

The 1100s saw clothing production undergoing transition. People began to form guilds, or simple unions of men and women doing the same work, and individuals set up shops as shoemakers, weavers, and tailors. Under the guidance of the weavers' guild, the quality of cloth improved. Tailors began to cut and stitch garments into vests, shirts, and trousers for men. Women's shapeless tunics gave way to long dresses that were tightly fitted to the upper body. Clothes went from simple coverings for the body to the beginnings of fashionable apparel.

Today, clothing manufacture is one of the world's largest industries, and fashion—what to wear and how to wear it—is an important part of everyone's lives.

1. Recognizing Words in Context

Find the word *transition* in the passage. One definition below is a *synonym* for that word; it means the same or almost the same thing. One definition is an *antonym*; it has the opposite or nearly opposite meaning. The other has a completely different meaning. Label the definitions S for *synonym*, A for *antonym*, and D for *different*.

_____ a. change

_____ b. stability

_____ c. intensity

2. Distinguishing Fact from Opinion

Two of the statements below present *facts*, which can be proved correct. The other statement is an *opinion*, which expresses someone's thoughts or beliefs. Label the statements F for *fact* and O for *opinion*.

_____ a. People grew their own flax or raised sheep for wool.

_____ b. In the 1100s, people began to form guilds.

_____ c. Fashion is an important part of everyone's lives.

3. Keeping Events in Order

Label the statements below 1, 2, and 3 to show the order in which the events happened.

_____ a. Clothes consisted of cloth that was draped and tied on.

_____ b. Shapeless garments gave way to close-fitting ones.

_____ c. People began to form guilds.

4. Making Correct Inferences

Two of the statements below are correct *inferences,* or reasonable guesses. They are based on information in the passage. The other statement is an incorrect, or faulty, inference. Label the statements C for *correct* inference and F for *faulty* inference.

_____ a. Early people did not care how they looked.

_____ b. The rise of guilds changed the way clothing was made and worn.

_____ c. From its beginning as simple covering for the body, clothing has become a major concern.

5. Understanding Main Ideas

One of the statements below expresses the main idea of the passage. One statement is too general, or too broad. The other explains only part of the passage; it is too narrow. Label the statements M for *main idea,* B for *too broad,* and N for *too narrow.*

_____ a. Clothing, which for centuries was mostly unfitted, changed to fitted garments with the rise of the guild system.

_____ b. Today the clothing industry is one of the world's largest, and fashion is an important part of everyone's lives.

_____ c. Clothes have changed over the centuries.

Correct Answers, Part A _____

Correct Answers, Part B _____

Total Correct Answers _____

The Earth's Layers

The Earth's structure comprises three layers. The outermost layer, which covers the Earth like a thin skin, is called the crust. Beneath it is a thick layer called the mantle, and occupying the innermost region is the core.

The crust is thicker in some places than in others. Under the oceans, the crust, called oceanic crust, has an average thickness of 3 miles (5 kilometers). Under the continents, its average thickness is 19 miles (31 kilometers), although continental crust may be about 43 miles (70 kilometers) thick under some mountains. This difference in the crust's thickness is one of its distinctive characteristics.

Another difference between oceanic and continental crust is the kinds of rocks each has. Rocks found under the continents are less dense than those found mostly in the ocean basins. However, the basaltic type of rock that covers most of the ocean floors also lies under parts of the continents.

The Earth's mantle is about 1,800 miles (2,900 kilometers) thick and is divided into regions. The rocky upper mantle material near the crust is quite rigid. But if pressure were applied to it over millions of years, it would become slightly more elastic. The lower mantle near Earth's core has rocks with more elasticity; they are soft and pliable. Scientists have identified areas about 200 miles (320 kilometers) wide between the lower mantle and the outer core that are denser than the surrounding regions.

The core extends outward from the Earth's center to a radius of about 2,160 miles (3,480 kilometers). Obtaining information about the Earth's interior is so difficult that many ideas about its structure remain uncertain. Some evidence indicates that the core is divided into zones. The inner core, with a radius of about 780 miles (1,255 kilometers), is quite rigid and may consist mainly of heavy metals such as iron; but the outer core, which surrounds it, is almost liquid and may be mostly melted iron and nickel.

Theory suggests that the density of the inner core is about 9 to 12 ounces per cubic inch (16 to 20 grams per cubic centimeter). The density of the outer core is about 6 to 7 ounces per cubic inch (11 to 12 grams per cubic centimeter). However, scientific study of Earth's structure is based largely on seismic wave data, so scientists sometimes disagree about the description of Earth's interior since it cannot be studied directly.

Reading Time _____

Recalling Facts

1. The Earth's three layers, from innermost to outermost, are the
   - ❏ a. core, mantle, and crust.
   - ❏ b. mantle, core, and crust.
   - ❏ c. crust, mantle, and core.

2. The Earth's crust is much thicker under
   - ❏ a. oceans.
   - ❏ b. the mantle.
   - ❏ c. continents.

3. The Earth's mantle is about
   - ❏ a. 500 miles thick.
   - ❏ b. 1,000 miles thick.
   - ❏ c. 1,800 miles thick.

4. The Earth's upper mantle is
   - ❏ a. very elastic.
   - ❏ b. quite rigid.
   - ❏ c. both elastic and rigid.

5. The kind of rock that covers most of the ocean floors is
   - ❏ a. iron.
   - ❏ b. basaltic.
   - ❏ c. nickel.

Understanding Ideas

6. The Earth's core is still somewhat of a mystery because
   - ❏ a. no one has studied it.
   - ❏ b. only indirect information is available.
   - ❏ c. it is impossible to obtain information about it.

7. Of the three basic layers of the Earth, the thickest layer is the
   - ❏ a. crust.
   - ❏ b. mantle.
   - ❏ c. core.

8. If theories about the core are correct, you can conclude that the difference in density between the inner and outer cores is due to the
   - ❏ a. difference in the state of material that comprises each.
   - ❏ b. seismic wave data.
   - ❏ c. process of erosion.

9. It is likely that scientists will
   - ❏ a. always disagree about the structure of the Earth's core.
   - ❏ b. continue to study the Earth's core.
   - ❏ c. soon resolve their differences about the Earth's core.

10. A comparison of the densities of the inner and outer core material suggests that
    - ❏ a. they are about the same.
    - ❏ b. the outer core is slightly more dense.
    - ❏ c. the inner core is slightly more dense.

A Journey to the Center of the Earth

By the nineteenth century, science had shown that the Earth must be a solid body. However, in 1864, this did not stop French author Jules Verne from writing a novel titled *Journey to the Center of the Earth.* In it, the narrator, Harry; his uncle, Professor von Hardwigg; and a guide named Hans descend into the interior of the Earth through an opening in a volcanic crater.

Verne did not let science spoil this great adventure. He was probably unaware that the force of gravity slowly weakens, reaching zero at the center of the Earth. As for increasing air pressure with depth, Verne simply said that the increase would be so gradual that his explorers would become accustomed to it. Verne did touch on the problem of the Earth's internal heat, but his explorers find it does not go beyond a safe limit. We know that the Earth's interior must be totally dark, but Verne's explorers find it well lighted by a mysterious "electrical influence."

Because the Earth's interior as explained by Verne is not totally inhospitable, Harry, his uncle, and Hans are free to have amazing adventures within the Earth. At the Earth's center, they find a vast sea—complete with sea monsters! Caught in a volcanic eruption, they are carried upward by the lava flow and propelled out of the Earth's interior like circus performers fired from a cannon!

1. Recognizing Words in Context

Find the word *force* in the passage. One definition below is a *synonym* for that word; it means the same or almost the same thing. One definition is an *antonym;* it has the opposite or nearly opposite meaning. The other has a completely different meaning. Label the definitions S for *synonym*, A for *antonym*, and D for *different*.

_____ a. strength

_____ b. compel

_____ c. weakness

2. Distinguishing Fact from Opinion

Two of the statements below present *facts,* which can be proved correct. The other statement is an *opinion,* which expresses someone's thoughts or beliefs. Label the statements F for *fact* and O for *opinion.*

_____ a. Gravity reaches zero at the center of the Earth.

_____ b. The idea of a journey to the center of the Earth is silly.

_____ c. The Earth's interior is hot and dark.

3. Keeping Events in Order

Label the statements below 1, 2, and 3 to show the order in which the events happened.

_____ a. They discover a sea at the center of the Earth.

_____ b. The explorers descend into the Earth through a volcanic crater.

_____ c. The explorers are caught in a volcanic eruption.

4. Making Correct Inferences

Two of the statements below are correct *inferences,* or reasonable guesses. They are based on information in the passage. The other statement is an incorrect, or faulty, inference. Label the statements C for *correct* inference and F for *faulty* inference.

_____ a. Jules Verne wanted to entertain his readers, not inform them.

_____ b. Jules Verne was ignorant of all facts about the Earth's interior.

_____ c. Jules Verne knew that such a journey was impossible.

5. Understanding Main Ideas

One of the statements below expresses the main idea of the passage. One statement is too general, or too broad. The other explains only part of the passage; it is too narrow. Label the statements M for *main idea,* B for *too broad,* and N for *too narrow.*

_____ a. French author Jules Verne wrote novels with fantastic settings.

_____ b. Jules Verne wrote a novel about a journey to the center of the Earth.

_____ c. According to Verne, the Earth's interior was lighted by a mysterious "electrical influence."

Correct Answers, Part A _____

Correct Answers, Part B _____

Total Correct Answers _____

6 A Grasshoppers

Grasshoppers, close relatives of crickets, belong to two separate families of insects. The long-horned grasshoppers with long, thin antennae belong to one family, and the short-horned grasshoppers with short, thick antennae belong to another. Most common varieties of grasshoppers are short-horned grasshoppers.

Although some of the more than 5,000 species of grasshopper are wingless, most have well-developed wings. Grasshoppers usually fly only short distances; but when forced to migrate in search of food, they can fly in "short hops" that total hundreds of miles (kilometers).

The type of short-horned grasshoppers known as locusts are among the world's worst insect pests. About 10 different species have been known to form enormous migratory swarms that can cause agricultural havoc. Throughout history, great locust swarms have devastated crops and natural vegetation around the world.

According to some reports, a swarm of grasshoppers appears on the horizon like a black storm, creating a thundering roar with beating wings. After they land, the grasshoppers eat every living plant in sight before moving on. The use of pesticides have controlled swarming in most agriculturally developed areas of the world, but locust swarms are still a problem in many areas. Surprisingly, the same species that causes such problems in great numbers will often go for years living a peaceful, inconspicuous existence.

Unlike the swarming locusts, most grasshoppers lead solitary lives, joining others only for mating. Before laying its eggs in the late summer and fall, the female bores holes 1 to 2 inches (2.5 to 5 centimeters) deep in the soil of fields or grassy areas. There she deposits a mass of eggs that may total only a few eggs or may number more than a hundred. She covers the eggs with a frothy substance that hardens and forms a protective pod and also provides air space for the young grasshoppers when they hatch underground. A single female may lay several egg masses, each in a different hole, sometimes up to 20 pods in a season.

As winter approaches, adult grasshoppers die, and the young pass the winter in the egg stage. When the eggs hatch in the spring, the youngsters quickly work their way to the surface. The newly hatched grasshoppers look like miniature adults with big heads and long legs, but with undeveloped wings. They begin to eat green plants, grow rapidly, and molt five times in about six weeks, finally emerging as fully developed adults.

Reading Time _____

Recalling Facts

1. Locusts are a type of
   - ❏ a. cricket.
   - ❏ b. long-horned grasshopper.
   - ❏ c. short-horned grasshopper.

2. Grasshoppers usually
   - ❏ a. do not fly.
   - ❏ b. fly only short distances.
   - ❏ c. fly long distances.

3. Most grasshoppers live
   - ❏ a. as social insects.
   - ❏ b. in swarms.
   - ❏ c. solitary lives.

4. The female grasshopper lays
   - ❏ a. one egg a season.
   - ❏ b. one egg mass a season.
   - ❏ c. up to 20 egg masses a season.

5. Grasshoppers hatch in
   - ❏ a. spring.
   - ❏ b. summer.
   - ❏ c. fall.

Understanding Ideas

6. You can conclude from the article that all species of grasshoppers
   - ❏ a. are insect pests.
   - ❏ b. are alike in their appearance and habits.
   - ❏ c. differ greatly in their appearance and habits.

7. Locusts are a problem
   - ❏ a. in areas where food is scarce.
   - ❏ b. where pesticides are not used to control them.
   - ❏ c. in most agriculturally developed areas of the world.

8. As a rule, grasshoppers live
   - ❏ a. less than a year.
   - ❏ b. about one year.
   - ❏ c. for many years.

9. You can conclude that grasshoppers are
   - ❏ a. insects that have existed for a long time.
   - ❏ b. a new species of insects.
   - ❏ c. a new problem in agricultural areas.

10. The article suggests that grasshoppers are found
   - ❏ a. mostly in the United States.
   - ❏ b. around the world.
   - ❏ c. only in agriculturally developed areas.

The Grasshopper and the Ants (An Aesop Fable)

All through the warm, wonderful days of summer, Grasshopper danced in the fields and sang his sweet song. Grasshopper enjoyed life and was never hungry, for he had fields full of seeds and sweet, green grass to feast on.

Day after day, Grasshopper lazily watched the ants toil. The ants busily spent their days gathering food and struggling under the weight of the seeds and grains that they carried to their nest. Grasshopper wondered why the ants so foolishly spent their days working when they could be enjoying the lazy days of summer.

Soon, however, winter came with its cold and snow, and Grasshopper no longer had time to dance and sing. With so little food available, Grasshopper now spent his days desperately searching for food and soon became too weak and hungry to sing even the tiniest song.

Then Grasshopper remembered the ants and how hard they had worked during the summer. Surely, they would have food to share, and so Grasshopper dragged himself to a large ant nest and pleaded, "Please, help me for I'm cold and hungry, and there is no food anywhere to be found. Will you take me in and give me something to eat?"

"Last summer, we worked tirelessly to gather food while you played," the ants said. "You should have thought about what would happen when winter came," they scolded, and with that comment, they went back down into their nest.

1. **Recognizing Words in Context**
   Find the word *hard* in the passage. One definition below is a *synonym* for that word; it means the same or almost the same thing. One definition is an *antonym;* it has the opposite or nearly opposite meaning. The other has a completely different meaning. Label the definitions S for *synonym,* A for *antonym,* and D for *different.*

   _____ a. difficult

   _____ b. easily

   _____ c. strenuously

2. **Distinguishing Fact from Opinion**
   Two of the statements below present *facts,* which can be proved correct. The other statement is an *opinion,* which expresses someone's thoughts or beliefs. Label the statements F for *fact* and O for *opinion.*

   _____ a. Grasshopper was foolish not to think about winter.

   _____ b. During the summer, the ants gathered food for the coming winter.

   _____ c. Grasshopper danced and sang all summer long.

3. Keeping Events in Order

Two of the statements below describe events that happened at the same time. The other statement describes an event that happened before or after those events. Label them S for *same time*, B for *before*, and A for *after*.

_____ a. Grasshopper danced and sang in the fields.

_____ b. The ants gathered food and carried it back to their nest.

_____ c. The ants refused to give Grasshopper any food.

4. Making Correct Inferences

Two of the statements below are correct *inferences*, or reasonable guesses. They are based on information in the passage. The other statement is an incorrect, or faulty, inference. Label the statements C for *correct* inference and F for *faulty* inference.

_____ a. The ants were smarter than Grasshopper.

_____ b. Grasshoppers do not store food for the winter.

_____ c. Grasshopper was going to starve to death.

5. Understanding Main Ideas

One of the statements below expresses the main idea of the passage. One statement is too general, or too broad. The other explains only part of the passage; it is too narrow. Label the statements M for *main idea*, B for *too broad*, and N for *too narrow*.

_____ a. Grasshopper learns a lesson from the ants about planning for the future.

_____ b. Grasshoppers and ants, while both are insects, have many differences.

_____ c. During the summer, the ants gathered and stored food.

Correct Answers, Part A _____

Correct Answers, Part B _____

Total Correct Answers _____

Living Arrangements

Close living arrangements between two different species is called symbiosis. The word *symbiosis* comes from the Greek word meaning "state of living together." Usually in symbiotic relationships, two organisms have a close physical contact, with one living on or in the other. In some cases, however, the relationship is less intimate. These relationships can range from mutually beneficial to harmful for one of the species.

Sometimes both organisms benefit from mutual relationships that exist among animals, plants, and microorganisms. For example, some plants are pollinated by insects, that in turn obtain food in the form of pollen or nectar from the plants. Many animals, including humans, have protozoans and bacteria that break down cellulose and other substances in the intestines. The resulting compounds are used by both the host and the microorganisms. In other cases, mutualism can exist between two animal species. African tick birds, for example, obtain food by cleaning parasites from the skin of giraffes, zebras, and other game animals.

In one type of relationship, one member benefits while the other is neither helped nor harmed. For example, the remora fish can attach itself to a shark, whale, or large turtle and be carried from meal to meal, feeding on scraps scattered by its host. The remora doesn't harm or help its host. Spiny and barbed seeds also form relationships with animals and humans that ensure the survival of the plants that produce the seeds. By attaching themselves to fur, feathers, or clothing, the seeds are carried long distances before they are dislodged. In this manner, some plants may be transported across continents and oceans.

A parasitic member of a relationship benefits while the host is harmed. Nearly all species of plants and animals are subject to at least one but usually several species of parasites. Parasites can be transferred from host to host in complicated life cycles that involve more than one host.

Parasites generally absorb food from their hosts but may also receive water, minerals, and shelter. Most parasites are pathogens that cause diseases such as typhoid fever, cholera, malaria, polio, and influenza in humans. If a host dies prematurely from disease, however, the parasite is also at risk of dying. As a result, many parasites and their hosts have evolved a form of mutual tolerance, in which, nevertheless, the host is still harmed in some way, sometimes even fatally.

Reading Time _____

Recalling Facts

1. Symbiosis is a close living arrangement
   - ❏ a. between two of the same species.
   - ❏ b. between two different species.
   - ❏ c. that involves two hosts.

2. Symbiotic relationships
   - ❏ a. are always mutually beneficial.
   - ❏ b. may be harmful to one party.
   - ❏ c. may be harmful to both parties.

3. The remora fish
   - ❏ a. harms its host.
   - ❏ b. helps its host.
   - ❏ c. neither harms nor helps its host.

4. In a symbiotic relationship, a parasite is the organism that
   - ❏ a. benefits.
   - ❏ b. is harmed.
   - ❏ c. is killed.

5. An example of a mutually beneficial symbiotic relationship is
   - ❏ a. plants that must be pollinated by insects.
   - ❏ b. seeds that attach to the fur of an insect.
   - ❏ c. the parasite that causes malaria.

Understanding Ideas

6. Parasites should be considered
   - ❏ a. dangerous to humans.
   - ❏ b. helpful to humans.
   - ❏ c. neutral organisms.

7. Seeds that attach to clothing and are dislodged are likely to
   - ❏ a. be dispersed widely.
   - ❏ b. never grow and produce plants.
   - ❏ c. be found in very limited areas.

8. The article suggests that
   - ❏ a. all symbiotic relationships are dangerous.
   - ❏ b. some symbiotic relationships are harmful.
   - ❏ c. no symbiotic relationship is harmful.

9. If a bird eats and expels the seeds of a berry that then sprout in a new location, the bird is
   - ❏ a. harming the plant.
   - ❏ b. neither harming or helping.
   - ❏ c. helping the plant.

10. You can conclude from the article that mutual tolerance between host and parasite
    - ❏ a. is beneficial to both.
    - ❏ b. should be avoided by the host.
    - ❏ c. should be avoided by the parasite.

7   B   Under the Mistletoe

The Druids, pagan priests who lived in ancient Britain and France, saw mistletoe growing high in the branches of oak trees. They noticed that when winter came and the giant oaks lost their leaves, the mistletoe remained green and fresh. Because the Druids thought mistletoe had magical powers, they attributed many wondrous things to it. They thought that it could cure diseases, reconcile arguments, keep away harmful spirits, and even prevent nightmares. Because they believed it had great powers, the Druids considered mistletoe and the oaks on which it lived sacred.

Later, because it was always green, people began to gather mistletoe and use it as a cheerful decoration in midwinter. The tradition that mistletoe could heal wounds—even the wounds of a broken heart from a failed romance—eventually led to the tradition of kissing under the mistletoe.

Today, people know that mistletoe is not a magical plant. In fact, its berries are poisonous. It is not a romantic plant but a parasite—a plant that makes some of its own food but obtains its water and minerals from its host plant, usually the oak tree. Still, the tradition of using mistletoe as a holiday decoration persists, a legacy of the Druids of long ago.

1. Recognizing Words in Context

Find the word *reconcile* in the passage. One definition below is a *synonym* for that word; it means the same or almost the same thing. One definition is an *antonym;* it has the opposite or nearly opposite meaning. The other has a completely different meaning. Label the definitions S for *synonym,* A for *antonym,* and D for *different.*

_____ a. bring into harmony

_____ b. do again

_____ c. cause to flare up

2. Distinguishing Fact from Opinion

Two of the statements below present *facts,* which can be proved correct. The other statement is an *opinion,* which expresses someone's thoughts or beliefs. Label the statements F for *fact* and O for *opinion.*

_____ a. Mistletoe is a parasite.

_____ b. Mistletoe can heal wounds and sadness.

_____ c. People use mistletoe as a midwinter decoration.

3. Keeping Events in Order

Label the statements below 1, 2, and 3 to show the order in which the events happened.

_____ a. Druids believed that mistletoe had magical powers.

_____ b. People learned that mistletoe was poisonous.

_____ c. People began to kiss under the mistletoe.

4. Making Correct Inferences

Two of the statements below are correct *inferences,* or reasonable guesses. They are based on information in the passage. The other statement is an incorrect, or faulty, inference. Label the statements C for *correct* inference and F for *faulty* inference.

_____ a. Mistletoe has many traditions associated with it.

_____ b. Mistletoe has long been used as a winter decoration.

_____ c. Mistletoe is completely harmless.

5. Understanding Main Ideas

One of the statements below expresses the main idea of the passage. One statement is too general, or too broad. The other explains only part of the passage; it is too narrow. Label the statements M for *main idea,* B for *too broad,* and N for *too narrow.*

_____ a. The Druids of ancient Britain and France considered mistletoe sacred.

_____ b. Mistletoe, a parasite of the oak tree, has a history of ancient traditions and beliefs.

_____ c. Some plants have traditions attached to them.

Correct Answers, Part A _____

Correct Answers, Part B _____

Total Correct Answers _____

Copper, the First Metal

The wires that deliver electricity for power and many of the wires that carry telephone messages are made of copper. So are the wires in electric motors and generators and the circuits in radios, television sets, computers, and other electronic devices. Copper is used because, aside from expensive silver, it is the best metal for conducting electricity.

Copper was the first metal humans used for tools and implements, probably because copper, like gold and silver, is sometimes found in a pure state and can be beaten into shape even when cold. The Egyptians and the Sumerians may have used copper about 7,000 years ago. The metal was named for the island of Cyprus, where the Romans obtained their supply of copper. American Indians made copper beads and tools long before Europeans arrived in the Americas. Bronze, an alloy of copper and tin, was used so generally in early history that one period is known as the Bronze Age; and brass, an alloy of copper and zinc, was used in Roman times. Copper and bronze were the most important metals until steel was first produced.

In the United States, copper was first mined at Simsbury, Connecticut, in about 1709. Large-scale mining began in 1845 in the Michigan deposits near Lake Superior. Today Arizona, Utah, New Mexico, and Montana produce about 90 percent of the ore mined in the United States, and Nevada, Michigan, Tennessee, and Missouri provide most of the remainder. In the United States, copper production ranges from 1 million to 1.5 million tons (900,000–1,300,000 metric tons) a year, and between 40 and 50 percent of the copper produced is reclaimed metal.

Copper is easily worked and is remarkably ductile. It can be cold-rolled down to one one-thousandth inch in thickness; and by cold drawing, its length can be increased as much as 5,000 times. Hence, copper is an ideal metal for making wire. It has pleasing color and luster, takes a high polish, and forms alloys readily with almost all metals. For cooking utensils, copper is coated with tin to prevent the formation of harmful compounds.

About one-half of the copper used in the United States is for electrical equipment. Another third is used to fashion products such as pipe, tubing, and other plumbing fixtures, hardware, and machine tool products. Its versatility makes copper useful to the transportation industry and for refrigeration equipment. It has many other miscellaneous uses.

Reading Time _____

Recalling Facts

1. Copper gets its name from
   - ❏ a. beads made by American Indians.
   - ❏ b. its color.
   - ❏ c. the island of Cyprus.

2. Bronze is composed of copper and
   - ❏ a. zinc.
   - ❏ b. silver.
   - ❏ c. tin.

3. Copper is most often used for
   - ❏ a. transportation equipment.
   - ❏ b. electrical equipment.
   - ❏ c. plumbing fixtures.

4. In the United States, copper was first mined in
   - ❏ a. Michigan.
   - ❏ b. Connecticut.
   - ❏ c. Montana.

5. Humans first used copper to make
   - ❏ a. jewelry.
   - ❏ b. tools.
   - ❏ c. clothing.

Understanding Ideas

6. It is likely that copper costs
   - ❏ a. less than silver.
   - ❏ b. more than silver.
   - ❏ c. the same as silver.

7. You can conclude from the article that an alloy
   - ❏ a. is metal in its pure state.
   - ❏ b. consists of more than one metal.
   - ❏ c. always includes copper.

8. The article suggests that copper's importance stems from its
   - ❏ a. beauty.
   - ❏ b. usefulness.
   - ❏ c. longevity.

9. You can conclude from the article that pure copper
   - ❏ a. should not be used in cooking utensils.
   - ❏ b. is useless unless it is coated.
   - ❏ c. is dangerous to humans.

10. The article indicates that copper production
    - ❏ a. is decreasing in the United States.
    - ❏ b. takes place mostly in the eastern United States.
    - ❏ c. is a major industry in the United States.

Pity the Poor Penny

In 1900, when a quart of milk cost eight cents, copper pennies were valuable coins, but today, many people consider them a nuisance. Many pennies end up in jars or are dropped and forgotten. On the other hand, if a bill comes to $9.99, people usually want that penny change. Sales taxes and discounts create odd numbers that keep pennies in circulation.

That penny in your pocket originated at the United States Bureau of the Mint, where strips of copper alloy pass through machine presses that punch out small disks. A second machine heats and rolls the disks to give them rims, and then the disks go into a coin press that stamps the head and tail designs onto them simultaneously.

Inspectors check every penny to see that it has been perfectly struck. An off-center design, a double impression, or a blank are all coveted collectors' items, and the mint tries to make sure that their mistakes never leave the premises.

The gleaming new pennies are counted, wrapped in paper rolls, and sent off to banks. From there, the penny rolls are distributed to businesses where they go into cash drawers to make change—and more pennies in your pocket.

1. Recognizing Words in Context

Find the word *coveted* in the passage. One definition below is a *synonym* for that word; it means the same or almost the same thing. One definition is an *antonym;* it has the opposite or nearly opposite meaning. The other has a completely different meaning. Label the definitions S for *synonym*, A for *antonym*, and D for *different*.

_____ a. desired

_____ b. unwanted

_____ c. interesting

2. Distinguishing Fact from Opinion

Two of the statements below present *facts,* which can be proved correct. The other statement is an *opinion,* which expresses someone's thoughts or beliefs. Label the statements F for *fact* and O for *opinion.*

_____ a. Inspectors check every penny to see that it is perfect.

_____ b. Many people consider pennies a nuisance.

_____ c. In 1900, a quart of milk cost eight cents.

3. Keeping Events in Order

Label the statements below 1, 2, and 3 to show the order in which the events happened.

_____ a. A machine cuts small disks out of a sheet of copper.

_____ b. The new pennies are distributed to banks.

_____ c. The head and tail designs are stamped onto the disks.

4. Making Correct Inferences

Two of the statements below are correct *inferences*, or reasonable guesses. They are based on information in the passage. The other statement is an incorrect, or faulty, inference. Label the statements C for *correct* inference and F for *faulty* inference.

_____ a. Pennies have a place in today's business world.

_____ b. Pennies should be discarded.

_____ c. Most people today do not value pennies very highly.

5. Understanding Main Ideas

One of the statements below expresses the main idea of the passage. One statement is too general, or too broad. The other explains only part of the passage; it is too narrow. Label the statements M for *main idea*, B for *too broad*, and N for *too narrow*.

_____ a. Pennies are an American coin.

_____ b. Pennies are made from strips of copper alloy that are cut, rolled, and stamped to create coins.

_____ c. A copper penny, although not much valued, is produced and distributed by means of careful processes.

Correct Answers, Part A _____

Correct Answers, Part B _____

Total Correct Answers _____

General George Armstrong Custer, the leader of "Custer's Last Stand," has been defended as a war hero and criticized as a showy glory seeker. This is because of conflicting stories about his final battle at Little Bighorn.

George Armstrong Custer, the son of a farmer and blacksmith, was born on December 5, 1839, in Ohio. Young Custer wanted to be a soldier and received an appointment to West Point, where he was a careless student and graduated at the bottom of his class.

Assigned to the Second Cavalry, Custer fought in the Civil War battle of Bull Run and, in June 1863, was given the wartime rank of brigadier general. He served gallantly at Gettysburg and in the Virginia campaigns and was rewarded with the rank of major general and command of the Third Cavalry Division.

After the war, Custer returned to his regular rank as captain. Rash and headstrong, he was soon in trouble with his superiors and even offended President Grant by condemning the War Department's Indian policy. Only favorable public opinion convinced the higher command to allow Custer to take part in an expedition being organized against the Sioux.

The expedition left Fort Lincoln, North Dakota, in May 1876 under General Alfred H. Terry. It was directed against the forces assembled by Sioux chiefs Crazy Horse and Sitting Bull in Montana. On June 24, scouts reported a Sioux village in a bend of the Little Bighorn River, and Terry sent Custer's troops to prevent the Sioux from escaping. Custer, believing the Sioux were few in number, decided to disregard his orders, and he sent a detachment under Captain Frederick Benteen toward the left to explore the area south of the river bend. Soon afterward, Custer sighted the village and ordered Major Marcus A. Reno's troops to approach the Indian camp along the river's west bank.

Sitting Bull's forces numbered about 6,000. Most of them lay in ambush in the hills around the village. Reno's forces were quickly driven back with a loss of 56 soldiers. Benteen, hearing gunfire, hurried to Reno's aid.

When Terry's troops arrived the next day, they had no word from Custer and the Sioux were gone. On a slope west of the village, Terry's troops found the bodies of Custer and the more than 200 soldiers who had followed him into battle. Of Custer's troops, only an Indian scout escaped the battle alive.

Reading Time _____

Recalling Facts

1. As a young man, Custer wanted to be a
   - ❑ a. teacher.
   - ❑ b. minister.
   - ❑ c. soldier.

2. As a student, Custer was considered
   - ❑ a. careless.
   - ❑ b. brilliant but lazy.
   - ❑ c. dedicated.

3. In June 1863, Custer was given the wartime rank of
   - ❑ a. captain.
   - ❑ b. brigadier general.
   - ❑ c. major general.

4. Custer offended President Grant by disagreeing about
   - ❑ a. Civil War strategy.
   - ❑ b. economic policies.
   - ❑ c. the War Department's Indian policy.

5. In the expedition against the Sioux, Custer was ordered to
   - ❑ a. attack the Indians.
   - ❑ b. make peace with the Indians.
   - ❑ c. bar the Indians' escape.

Understanding Ideas

6. In disregarding his orders at Little Bighorn, Custer
   - ❑ a. acted out of character.
   - ❑ b. acted true to character.
   - ❑ c. did what was best for his troops.

7. Custer's biggest mistake at Little Bighorn was
   - ❑ a. overestimating the number of Indian forces.
   - ❑ b. ignoring the number of Indian forces.
   - ❑ c. underestimating the number of Indian forces.

8. Based on the article, you can conclude that Custer's historical reputation
   - ❑ a. should be reconsidered.
   - ❑ b. is firmly established.
   - ❑ c. may never be resolved.

9. Disregarding Terry's orders was an example of Custer's
   - ❑ a. great respect for authority.
   - ❑ b. rash and headstrong ways.
   - ❑ c. strong leadership skills.

10. Custer died with 200 of his troops, which suggests that
    - ❑ a. Custer's troops followed their leader's orders.
    - ❑ b. the troops were poor soldiers.
    - ❑ c. Custer expected to lose the battle.

9	B		Separate Tables

While students at the U.S. Military Academy at West Point, Pierce Young and George Armstrong Custer had been best friends, but during the Civil War, they were generals fighting on opposite sides. Custer fought for the Union, and Young, for the Confederacy.

One day, General Young was invited to have breakfast at the mansion of the Hunter family in Virginia, and as he sat down to the meal, a shell burst nearby. Looking out a window, Young saw General Custer and his staff charging toward the house. "Tell Custer I leave this breakfast for him," Young told his hosts and then escaped through the window. Custer enjoyed the meal that Young abandoned.

During the day, Young's troops drove the Union forces back, and by dinnertime, Young was again in sight of the Hunter mansion. Inside, Custer was about to sit down to dinner. When he heard the commotion made by the arriving Confederate forces, Custer laughed. "That's Pierce Young coming back," he remarked to the Hunters. "I knew he wouldn't leave me here in peace. Tell him his old classmate leaves his love with his excellent dinner." As Young had done earlier that day, Custer left through the window. Young then marched into the Hunters' home, sat down, and enjoyed the fine meal that Custer had abandoned.

1. **Recognizing Words in Context**

Find the word *left* in the passage. One definition below is a *synonym* for that word; it means the same or almost the same thing. One definition is an *antonym;* it has the opposite or nearly opposite meaning. The other has a completely different meaning. Label the definitions S for *synonym*, A for *antonym*, and D for *different*.

_____ a. arrived

_____ b. opposite of *right*

_____ c. departed

2. **Distinguishing Fact from Opinion**

Two of the statements below present *facts*, which can be proved correct. The other statement is an *opinion*, which expresses someone's thoughts or beliefs. Label the statements F for *fact* and O for *opinion*.

_____ a. On that day, Custer and Young behaved like silly young boys.

_____ b. The two generals fought on opposite sides during the Civil War.

_____ c. General Young and General Custer had been classmates at West Point.

3. Keeping Events in Order

Two of the statements below describe events that happened at the same time. The other statement describes an event that happened before or after those events. Label them S for *same time*, B for *before*, and A for *after*.

_____ a. General Young was sitting down to breakfast.

_____ b. Young drove the Union forces back.

_____ c. A shell burst nearby.

4. Making Correct Inferences

Two of the statements below are correct *inferences*, or reasonable guesses. They are based on information in the passage. The other statement is an incorrect, or faulty, inference. Label the statements C for *correct* inference and F for *faulty* inference.

_____ a. Young and Custer did not let their former friendship interfere with their duties.

_____ b. Young and Custer did not take their roles as opposing generals seriously.

_____ c. Both Custer and Young had a sense of humor.

5. Understanding Main Ideas

One of the statements below expresses the main idea of the passage. One statement is too general, or too broad. The other explains only part of the passage; it is too narrow. Label the statements M for *main idea*, B for *too broad*, and N for *too narrow*.

_____ a. Custer abandoned his dinner to General Young.

_____ b. General Young and General Custer swapped control of the Hunter mansion twice on the same day.

_____ c. During the Civil War, friends sometimes became enemies.

Correct Answers, Part A _____

Correct Answers, Part B _____

Total Correct Answers _____

48

Come Follow the Band

Although the word *band* can apply to any ensemble of musicians, originally the instruments played in a band were all from the same group, usually wind instruments. A band, as the term is most broadly understood, is one of two principal types: the marching band and the concert band.

A marching band plays only instruments that musicians can carry as they walk, and so the instruments are usually limited to wind and percussion instruments. The wind instruments most commonly used in marching bands are the flute and piccolo; the reeds, including the clarinet, saxophone, and other saxhorns; and the brass winds, including the cornet, trumpet, trombone, sousaphone, and tuba. The chief percussion instruments are drums, cymbals, and the triangle. Some marching bands also carry a glockenspiel.

A concert band is led by a conductor as is a symphony orchestra whereas a marching band is usually led by a drum major. The actual musical director of a marching band has a less conspicuous role. The drum major is traditionally a tall person of commanding stature who wears a uniform topped by a hat with a high crown and plume. The drum major often carries a baton to establish the beat for the band and, with the aid of a whistle, signals the various steps and turns in marching formation. In addition to the drum major, many marching bands include baton twirlers and a flag corps.

Marching formations have developed into such intricate and spectacular patterns that a good marching band must spend weeks practicing the marching steps as well as the music. The position of every band member is plotted on charts and memorized. College and university bands are especially noted for such ingenious formations as moving and intertwining letters of their teams' names and schools.

Because concert bands play while seated or in stationary formation, they can use a larger variety of instruments. In addition to those instruments played by marching bands, concert bands also use such instruments as the cello, double bass, timpani, harp, chimes, xylophone, and vibraphone.

A jazz band is made up of two distinct groups: a rhythm section most often consisting of drums, string bass (or tuba), guitar (or banjo), and piano or a selection of these; and a melody section most often consisting of trumpets, trombones, clarinets, and saxophones. Early New Orleans jazz bands were marching bands that played for parades, funerals, picnics, and parties.

Reading Time _____

Recalling Facts

1. Originally a band consisted of
   - ❑ a. any ensemble of musicians.
   - ❑ b. one group of instruments.
   - ❑ c. wind and percussion instruments.

2. A marching band
   - ❑ a. plays only instruments musicians can carry.
   - ❑ b. is led by a conductor.
   - ❑ c. is made up of two distinct groups.

3. Reed instruments include
   - ❑ a. trombones and tubas.
   - ❑ b. clarinets and saxophones.
   - ❑ c. flutes and drums.

4. Concert bands can use a larger variety of instruments than marching bands because
   - ❑ a. concert musicians are better trained.
   - ❑ b. concert musicians play while seated.
   - ❑ c. concert bands are bigger.

5. A jazz band is made up of
   - ❑ a. a rhythm section and a melody section.
   - ❑ b. percussion instruments.
   - ❑ c. three musicians.

Understanding Ideas

6. You can conclude from the article that the meaning of the word *band*
   - ❑ a. has become more specific over time.
   - ❑ b. has not changed over time.
   - ❑ c. has broadened over the years.

7. The cello is not part of a marching band because it is
   - ❑ a. too hard to play.
   - ❑ b. not loud enough.
   - ❑ c. a large, hard-to-carry instrument.

8. The person most likely to attract attention in a marching band is the
   - ❑ a. drum major.
   - ❑ b. tuba player.
   - ❑ c. flag carrier.

9. A large, outdoor sporting event would most likely feature a
   - ❑ a. concert band.
   - ❑ b. marching band.
   - ❑ c. jazz band.

10. The article suggests that different types of bands evolved
    - ❑ a. to meet changing needs.
    - ❑ b. as new instruments were invented.
    - ❑ c. to provide more jobs for musicians.

10 B The March King

Born in Washington, D.C., in 1854, John Philip Sousa was a musical prodigy who could play almost any instrument. When he was only 13 years old, Sousa won a place in the United States Marine Band. Before he was 18, he had his own orchestra, and at 26, he returned to the Marine Band as its leader. In 1892, Sousa left the Marine Band to form his own group, Sousa's Band, which toured America and Europe.

Besides leading his bands, Sousa was composing some of the most stirring band music ever written. Almost everyone who has ever seen a parade or heard a marching band has heard a Sousa march: "The Washington Post March," "Semper Fidelis," "Hands Across the Sea," and many others.

In 1899, Sousa introduced a new band instrument—the sousaphone. He had noticed that tuba players, who provide the march's indispensable oom-pah, oom-pah beat, had trouble keeping in step because their tubas were so big and cumbersome. The sousaphone, which fits around the musician's body and rests on a shoulder, quickly replaced the tuba in marching bands and remains a standard band instrument today.

Sousa, beloved by all as America's March King, died in 1932. One of Sousa's best-known marches, "Stars and Stripes, Forever," remains a perennial favorite of Americans, who clap along as it is played at Fourth of July parades and concerts.

1. **Recognizing Words in Context**

   Find the word *prodigy* in the passage. One definition below is a *synonym* for that word; it means the same or almost the same thing. One definition is an *antonym*; it has the opposite or nearly opposite meaning. The other has a completely different meaning. Label the definitions S for *synonym*, A for *antonym*, and D for *different*.

   _____ a. failure

   _____ b. young genius

   _____ c. wanderer

2. **Distinguishing Fact from Opinion**

   Two of the statements below present *facts*, which can be proved correct. The other statement is an *opinion*, which expresses someone's thoughts or beliefs. Label the statements F for *fact* and O for *opinion*.

   _____ a. Sousa was beloved by all.

   _____ b. Sousa played in the Marine Band when he was 13 years old.

   _____ c. Sousa invented the sousaphone.

3. Keeping Events in Order

Label the statements below 1, 2, and 3 to show the order in which the events happened.

_____ a. Sousa introduced the sousaphone.

_____ b. Sousa left the Marine Band to form Sousa's Band.

_____ c. Sousa led his own orchestra.

4. Making Correct Inferences

Two of the statements below are correct *inferences,* or reasonable guesses. They are based on information in the passage. The other statement is an incorrect, or faulty, inference. Label the statements C for *correct* inference and F for *faulty* inference.

_____ a. The sousaphone is used in marching bands because it is easier to carry than the tuba.

_____ b. Sousa excelled as both a bandleader and a composer.

_____ c. Most of Sousa's accomplishments occurred before he was 30 years old.

5. Understanding Main Ideas

One of the statements below expresses the main idea of the passage. One statement is too general, or too broad. The other explains only part of the passage; it is too narrow. Label the statements M for *main idea,* B for *too broad,* and N for *too narrow.*

_____ a. John Philip Sousa was a major force in developing American band music.

_____ b. American band music is very popular.

_____ c. John Philip Sousa, the March King, invented the sousaphone.

Correct Answers, Part A _____

Correct Answers, Part B _____

Total Correct Answers _____

11   A   Going Up

The movement of people and freight within relatively confined areas such as office buildings, airport terminals, and large ships is usually accomplished by means of elevators, escalators, or moving sidewalks. Elevators, or lifts, carry passengers and freight up and down. Escalators are moving staircases from one story of a building to the next. Moving sidewalks carry people horizontally or at a slight incline.

When it became possible to construct tall, multistoried buildings in the nineteenth century, the need arose to move people and freight from one level to another. Staircases are not practical in tall buildings. The mechanism invented for such use was the elevator, and the invention of the elevator, moreover, made even taller buildings possible.

Most modern elevators are pulled from above by steel cables. A cable-hoisted elevator travels up and down inside a shaft, which has doors opening from within at each floor. Above the shaft in its own room is an electric motor with a governor to control speed. There is also a panel of switches and relays to control stopping, starting, and reversing. The steel cables that support the car are looped around a drum attached to the driving motor. The greater the weight in the car, the tighter the cables grip the drum; and from the drive mechanism, the cables drop down the depth of the elevator shaft, holding a heavy counterweight.

The first commercial installation of an electrically driven passenger elevator was in 1889 in the Demarest Building in New York City. This elevator used an electric motor to drive a winding drum in the basement. Push-button controls were introduced in 1894, and in 1915, automatic car leveling was introduced. This control took over at each floor to guide the car to a precisely positioned stop. Power control of doors was added shortly thereafter.

Most modern elevators are completely automatic. The earliest control system was the single push-button panel, allowing riders to control the car. Group-automatic operation of two or more cars keeps them spaced at specific intervals. This type of control is normally used in heavy traffic areas.

Today most elevators have inner and outer doors that will not operate unless both sets of doors are closed. There are usually photoelectric devices to keep doors from closing while passengers are entering or leaving. Because of the possibility of breakdowns, most elevators have alarm systems and a telephone that connects to an outside exchange.

Reading Time _____

Recalling Facts

1. Moving staircases are called
   - ❏ a. moving sidewalks.
   - ❏ b. elevators.
   - ❏ c. escalators.

2. Mechanisms used to carry people horizontally are called
   - ❏ a. moving sidewalks.
   - ❏ b. elevators.
   - ❏ c. escalators.

3. The Demarest Building in New York City had the
   - ❏ a. first commercially installed, electrically operated elevator.
   - ❏ b. the world's first elevator.
   - ❏ c. the first elevator with photoelectric devices.

4. Most modern elevators operate
   - ❏ a. by steering.
   - ❏ b. automatically.
   - ❏ c. manually.

5. The devices that help keep elevator doors from closing on passengers are
   - ❏ a. photoelectric devices.
   - ❏ b. group-automatic operating systems.
   - ❏ c. cable-hoisted elevator cars.

Understanding Ideas

6. Staircases are not practical in tall buildings because
   - ❏ a. people would be likely to fall.
   - ❏ b. stairs are expensive to build.
   - ❏ c. people would take too long to move from floor to floor.

7. The invention of the elevator made taller buildings possible because
   - ❏ a. construction costs plummeted.
   - ❏ b. it became easier to move people up and down.
   - ❏ c. elevators take up less room than stairs.

8. The advantage of completely automatic elevators is that
   - ❏ a. they are totally safe.
   - ❏ b. humans are not needed to operate them.
   - ❏ c. no maintenance is required.

9. In a three-story building, the most efficient way to transport passengers with strollers or in wheelchairs is
   - ❏ a. by escalator.
   - ❏ b. by elevator.
   - ❏ c. on moving sidewalks.

10. According to the article, modern elevators
    - ❏ a. are equipped with a multitude of safety features.
    - ❏ b. are frequently checked for problems.
    - ❏ c. will no doubt be updated in the near future.

The modern passenger elevator had its origins in 1854 when an American engineer named Elisha Graves Otis introduced the first fail-safe mechanism for a freight hoist. Previously, hoists had been extremely unsafe because the ropes used to lift freight on platforms frequently broke—sometimes killing people.

Somewhat of a showman, Otis demonstrated his safety hoist in a dramatic way at the Crystal Palace Exposition in New York City. Otis stood on a hoist platform filled with barrels, boxes, and other freight. The hoist was hauled up about thirty feet above the ground and then Otis ordered an assistant to cut the rope. On earlier hoists, this would have been a disastrous—and probably fatal—stunt. However, Otis's fail-safe mechanism worked. The hoist stopped completely after the rope was cut!

The key to Otis's device was a bow-shaped spring attached to the top of the hoist platform. Notched guide rails were set on either side of the hoist. When the rope of the hoist was cut, the spring flexed and its ends jammed in the guide rail notches, preventing the platform from falling.

Otis went on to install the world's first passenger elevator in 1857 at V. Haughwout & Company, a New York china store.

1. Recognizing Words in Context

Find the word *dramatic* in the passage. One definition below is a *synonym* for that word; it means the same or almost the same thing. One definition is an *antonym*; it has the opposite or nearly opposite meaning. The other has a completely different meaning. Label the definitions S for *synonym*, A for *antonym*, and D for *different*.

_____ a. unexciting

_____ b. sensational

_____ c. amusing

2. Distinguishing Fact from Opinion

Two of the statements below present *facts*, which can be proved correct. The other statement is an *opinion*, which expresses someone's thoughts or beliefs. Label the statements F for *fact* and O for *opinion*.

_____ a. Otis was something of a showman.

_____ b. Otis developed a safety device for freight hoists.

_____ c. Freight hoists were extremely dangerous.

3. Keeping Events in Order

Two of the statements below describe events that happened at the same time. The other statement describes an event that happened before or after those events. Label them S for *same time,* B for *before,* and A for *after.*

_____ a. The platform stopped completely.

_____ b. Otis stood on a hoist platform with freight.

_____ c. The platform was hoisted into the air.

4. Making Correct Inferences

Two of the statements below are correct *inferences,* or reasonable guesses. They are based on information in the passage. The other statement is an incorrect, or faulty, inference. Label the statements C for *correct* inference and F for *faulty* inference.

_____ a. Otis was confident that his safety device would work.

_____ b. Otis showed no concern for his own life.

_____ c. Without a safety device like the one Otis invented, high-rise elevators would not be possible.

5. Understanding Main Ideas

One of the statements below expresses the main idea of the passage. One statement is too general, or too broad. The other explains only part of the passage; it is too narrow. Label the statements M for *main idea,* B for *too broad,* and N for *too narrow.*

_____ a. The development of the passenger elevator depended on a series of inventions and improvements.

_____ b. The world's first passenger elevator was installed in a New York china store in 1857.

_____ c. Elisha Graves Otis invented a fail-safe mechanism for freight hoists that made passenger elevators possible.

Correct Answers, Part A _____

Correct Answers, Part B _____

Total Correct Answers _____

The Industrial Revolution

Most products that people in the industrialized nations use today are manufactured swiftly by the process of mass production. In mass production, people (and sometimes, robots) work on assembly lines operating power-driven machines. People of ancient and medieval times had no such products. They had to spend long, tedious hours of hand labor to produce even simple goods, and the energy they employed came wholly from their own and animals' muscles. The Industrial Revolution is the name given to the movement in which machines changed people's way of life as well as their methods of manufacture.

About the time of the American Revolution, the people of England began to use machines to make cloth and steam engines to run the machines. A little later, they invented locomotives. Productivity began a spectacular climb, and by 1850, most English workers labored in industrial towns. Great Britain became the workshop of the world, and from Britain, the Industrial Revolution spread to the United States.

The most important of the changes that brought about the Industrial Revolution were (1) the invention of machines to do the work of hand tools; (2) the use of steam, and later other kinds of power; and (3) the adoption of the factory system.

It is almost impossible to imagine what the world would be like if the effects of the Industrial Revolution were swept away. Electric lights would go out; automobiles and airplanes would vanish; and telephones, radios, and television would disappear. Most of the abundant stocks of goods in department stores would be gone. The children of the poor would receive little or no schooling and would work from dawn to dark on the farm or in the home. Before machines were invented, children had to work to help provide their families with enough food, clothing, and shelter for all.

This relatively sudden change in the way people lived and worked deserves to be called a revolution. The Industrial Revolution differs from a political revolution in its immediate impact on people's lives and in its long life. The Industrial Revolution did not come to an end as, for example, the French Revolution did. Instead, the Industrial Revolution grew more powerful each year as new inventions and manufacturing processes added to the efficiency of machines and increased productivity. Indeed, since World War I, the mechanization of industry has increased so enormously that another revolution in production is taking place.

Reading Time _____

Recalling Facts

1. The Industrial Revolution marked the change from
   - ❏ a. hand labor to machine production.
   - ❏ b. animal power to people power.
   - ❏ c. small manufacturing plants to large manufacturing plants.

2. The Industrial Revolution began in
   - ❏ a. England.
   - ❏ b. Australia.
   - ❏ c. the United States.

3. Early machines were powered by
   - ❏ a. electricity.
   - ❏ b. steam engines.
   - ❏ c. locomotives.

4. By 1850, most English working people worked
   - ❏ a. on farms.
   - ❏ b. at home.
   - ❏ c. in industrial towns.

5. Mass production involves
   - ❏ a. people on assembly lines using machines.
   - ❏ b the manufacture of machinery.
   - ❏ c. intensive hand labor.

Understanding Ideas

6. To the average person, the most important result of the Industrial Revolution was probably
   - ❏ a. better education.
   - ❏ b. an easier way of life.
   - ❏ c. a greater understanding of mass production.

7. Assembly-line production involves
   - ❏ a. one worker completing one product.
   - ❏ b. careful hand manufacturing of goods.
   - ❏ c. many workers completing one product.

8. Assembly lines emphasize
   - ❏ a. efficiency.
   - ❏ b. personal attention.
   - ❏ c. creativity.

9. The word *revolution* refers to
   - ❏ a. any change in lifestyle.
   - ❏ b. a sudden major change.
   - ❏ c. the use of machinery in industry.

10. You can conclude from the article that the Industrial Revolution
    - ❏ a. has come to an end.
    - ❏ b. will soon come to end.
    - ❏ c. continues to grow in power.

12 B — The Lowell Experiment

In the 1820s, a group of Boston capitalists came together to organize the first planned factory city in the United States. They were determined to create something better than the horrible, dark mills and slums of England. The result was the city of Lowell, Massachusetts, where tall brick mills lined the Merrimack River for a mile (1.6 kilometers) and were connected by 15 miles (24 kilometers) of canals. The many windows in the mills flooded the interiors with sunlight, and the neat streets of the city were well lighted.

To house the workers—mainly young women from farm families—the planners constructed comfortable boarding houses and hired older women to supervise the mill workers who lived there.

Workdays were long—from 5:00 A.M. until 7:30 P.M.—but the hours and work were no longer or harder than workdays on a farm. When they were not working, the young women formed what they called improvement clubs. They read and discussed books, took piano lessons, and even published a magazine. Their publication, *The Lowell Offering,* was the first magazine ever written entirely by women.

The Lowell experiment was a great success. One delighted worker wrote, "For the first time in this country woman's labor had a monetary value. . . . And thus a long upward step in our material civilization was taken."

---

1. **Recognizing Words in Context**

   Find the word *flooded* in the passage. One definition below is a *synonym* for that word; it means the same or almost the same thing. One definition is an *antonym;* it has the opposite or nearly opposite meaning. The other has a completely different meaning. Label the definitions S for *synonym,* A for *antonym,* and D for *different.*

   _____ a. emptied

   _____ b. filled

   _____ c. inundated

2. **Distinguishing Fact from Opinion**

   Two of the statements below present *facts,* which can be proved correct. The other statement is an *opinion,* which expresses someone's thoughts or beliefs. Label the statements F for *fact* and O for *opinion.*

   _____ a. The mills of Lowell were wonderful places in which to work.

   _____ b. Lowell, Massachusetts, was the first planned factory city in the United States.

   _____ c. Millworkers created the first magazine written exclusively by women.

3. Keeping Events in Order

Label the statements below 1, 2, and 3 to show the order in which the events happened.

_____ a. Boston capitalists got together to plan a factory city.

_____ b. The mills of Lowell were built along the Merrimack River.

_____ c. Mill workers formed improvement clubs in their spare time.

4. Making Correct Inferences

Two of the statements below are correct *inferences*, or reasonable guesses. They are based on information in the passage. The other statement is an incorrect, or faulty, inference. Label the statements C for *correct* inference and F for *faulty* inference.

_____ a. Working conditions in Lowell were far better than in English mills.

_____ b. Farm women were used to working long hours.

_____ c. All the mill workers were happy in their jobs.

5. Understanding Main Ideas

One of the statements below expresses the main idea of the passage. One statement is too general, or too broad. The other explains only part of the passage; it is too narrow. Label the statements M for *main idea*, B for *too broad*, and N for *too narrow*.

_____ a. The mills' many windows flooded the interiors with sunlight.

_____ b. Lowell, Massachusetts, the first planned factory city in the United States, provided pleasant working and living conditions for mill workers.

_____ c. One of the most important changes brought about by the Industrial Revolution was the adoption of the factory system.

Correct Answers, Part A _____

Correct Answers, Part B _____

Total Correct Answers _____

13　A　　　Change Is Good

Certain animals and plants develop characteristics that help them cope with their environment. This natural process is called adaptation. Traits developed through adaptation may help plants and animals obtain food or shelter, or they may provide protection and help in producing and protecting offspring. The better-adapted organisms tend to thrive, reproduce, and pass adaptations to the next generation, resulting in the evolution of more organisms that are better fitted to their environments.

Each organism is adapted to its mode of life in a general way and to its own distinct niche in special ways. A plant, for example, depends on its roots to anchor itself and to absorb water. It depends on its green leaves to use the sun's energy to manufacture food from inorganic chemicals. These are general adaptations, common to most plant life. In addition, certain species of plants possess special adaptations. The mistletoe, for example, is a parasitic plant. It lacks true roots but anchors itself to the branches of a tree from which it absorbs water and chemicals. In order to survive, the mistletoe must establish its parasitic relationship with a suitable tree. The mistletoe is also dependent upon insects to pollinate its flowers and birds to disseminate its seeds.

Many animals have adaptations that help them elude predators. Some insects may resemble a leaf or a twig. A chameleon's skin coloring changes so that it blends in with surroundings, and the coats of deer are colored to blend with their surroundings. A deer's behavior is also adaptive. It has the ability to remain absolutely still when an enemy is near.

Favorable adaptations may involve migration for survival under certain conditions of temperature. Some organisms can create part of their own environment, as warm-blooded mammals do. They have the ability to adjust body heat to maintain temperature despite changing weather. Some adaptations to temporary situations may be reversible, as when humans become suntanned.

Usually adaptations are an advantage, but sometimes an organism becomes so well adapted to a particular environment that it finds it difficult to adapt to new conditions. For example, the huia bird of New Zealand depended upon a close collaboration between male and female. The male chiseled holes in decaying wood with its stout beak, and the female reached in with her long, slender beak to capture grubs. When New Zealand was deforested, these birds could no longer feed and soon became extinct.

Reading Time _____

Recalling Facts

1. The results of adaptation are
   - ❑ a. more organisms that are better fitted to their environments.
   - ❑ b. fewer organisms that are adapted to their environments.
   - ❑ c. environments that change to suit the characteristics of organisms.

2. The mistletoe's parasitic relationship with trees is an example of
   - ❑ a. general adaptation.
   - ❑ b. special adaptation.
   - ❑ c. temporary adaptation.

3. An example of adaptations common to plants is
   - ❑ a. anchoring themselves in tree branches.
   - ❑ b. changing colors to avoid enemies.
   - ❑ c. depending on leaves to manufacture food.

4. To help them elude predators, deer have adapted by
   - ❑ a. remaining absolutely still.
   - ❑ b. changing their feeding habits.
   - ❑ c. running away.

5. The huia bird became extinct when
   - ❑ a. weather conditions changed dramatically in New Zealand.
   - ❑ b. New Zealand was deforested.
   - ❑ c. female birds began to migrate.

Understanding Ideas

6. You can conclude from the article that the huia bird became extinct because it
   - ❑ a. migrated to a new environment that could not support it.
   - ❑ b. could not adapt to changes in its environment.
   - ❑ c. adapted its diet to meet new conditions.

7. If a group of deer stands completely still in the woods when humans are nearby, the deer probably
   - ❑ a. consider them friends.
   - ❑ b. are ignoring them.
   - ❑ c. think of them as enemies.

8. Changes in a chameleon's skin color that help it blend in with surroundings are an example of a
   - ❑ a. physical adaptation.
   - ❑ b. behavioral characteristic.
   - ❑ c. general animal trait.

9. An example of an adaptive physical characteristic is
   - ❑ a. a duck's webbed feet.
   - ❑ b. the barking of a dog.
   - ❑ c. the migration of a bird.

10. Plants and animals that cannot adapt to changing conditions are likely to
   - ❑ a. overpopulate an area.
   - ❑ b. die out.
   - ❑ c. survive.

13　B　The Adaptable Coyote

When humans move into an area, wildlife is often endangered. Some species, however, seem to thrive. Take, for example, the coyote.

For the last century, Americans have been trying to control coyote populations. As people arrived on the western prairies with their garbage and livestock, the adaptable coyote began to be a genuine nuisance. Coyotes are dangerous to livestock, and sheep ranchers have long wanted them eradicated because they attack their lambs.

To control coyote populations, an animal control unit of the Department of Agriculture destroys about 75,000 coyotes a year, while private citizens and local agencies may kill as many as 400,000. Estimates are that over 20 million coyotes have been destroyed in this century.

The coyote's response to all this has been to thrive. When exterminators made headway, coyotes produced more young and extended their range. As people cut down trees and made "prairies" of their parks and backyards, coyotes moved in. Now coyotes roam from the canyons of Los Angeles to New England and have even been seen inside New York City limits. From their failure to control coyotes, people are now facing the fact that this ancient species is here to stay, and people must figure out ways to learn to live with the adaptable coyote.

1. **Recognizing Words in Context**

   Find the word *eradicated* in the passage. One definition below is a *synonym* for that word; it means the same or almost the same thing. One definition is an *antonym;* it has the opposite or nearly opposite meaning. The other has a completely different meaning. Label the definitions S for *synonym,* A for *antonym,* and D for *different.*

   _____ a. irritated
   _____ b. encouraged
   _____ c. eliminated

2. **Distinguishing Fact from Opinion**

   Two of the statements below present *facts,* which can be proved correct. The other statement is an *opinion,* which expresses someone's thoughts or beliefs. Label the statements F for *fact* and O for *opinion.*

   _____ a. Coyotes attack lambs.
   _____ b. Some animal species seem to thrive when humans move into their area.
   _____ c. Coyotes roam the canyons of Los Angeles.

3. Keeping Events in Order

Label the statements below 1, 2, and 3 to show the order in which the events happened.

_____ a. Sheep ranchers have long wanted to get rid of coyotes.

_____ b. Coyotes have extended their range.

_____ c. People who moved into the western plains found coyotes there.

4. Making Correct Inferences

Two of the statements below are correct *inferences*, or reasonable guesses. They are based on information in the passage. The other statement is an incorrect, or faulty, inference. Label the statements C for *correct* inference and F for *faulty* inference.

_____ a. Coyotes should be killed.

_____ b. Coyotes are extremely adaptable.

_____ c. Coyotes cannot be prevented from spreading across the country.

5. Understanding Main Ideas

One of the statements below expresses the main idea of the passage. One statement is too general, or too broad. The other explains only part of the passage; it is too narrow. Label the statements M for *main idea*, B for *too broad*, and N for *too narrow*.

_____ a. Some animals can adapt to human pressures more easily than others.

_____ b. By increasing its numbers and spreading its range, the coyote has proved extremely adaptable to human civilization.

_____ c. For the last century, people have been trying to control coyotes by killing them in large numbers.

Correct Answers, Part A _____

Correct Answers, Part B _____

Total Correct Answers _____

There is no landmark in the world more famous than the Eiffel Tower. Not only does it dominate the skyline of Paris, but it is also a landmark of building construction history.

When the French government was organizing the Centennial Exposition of 1889, a fair to commemorate the 100th anniversary of the French Revolution, the noted bridge engineer Alexandre-Gustave Eiffel was asked to design and build a structure to symbolize the occasion. His finished product aroused both praise and criticism and also a great deal of amazement.

Nothing like the Eiffel Tower, a 984-foot (300-meter) tower of open-lattice wrought iron, had ever before been built. Not until the Chrysler Building was completed in New York City in 1930 was there a taller structure in the world. The base of the tower consists of four semicircular arches, inspired by both artistic design and weight-bearing engineering considerations. Glass-walled elevators ascend on a curve up the legs of the tower to the first and second platforms. Two different pairs of elevators go from the second level to the third platform near the top. From this platform, the view extends for 50 miles (80 kilometers) on a clear day.

After the 1889 fair closed, Eiffel realized that the only way to save his monument would be to find new and profitable uses for it. He supervised changes to accommodate a meteorological station and a military telegraph station. Further modifications were made for the expositions of 1900, 1925, and 1937.

For many years, management of the Eiffel Tower was in the hands of a public firm, but in 1981, the city government of Paris took over its management. The tower underwent extensive renovation and reconstruction in preparation for its 100th anniversary in 1989. The renovation stripped off paint down to the girders, removed the excess weight of structures on the upper levels, and built new lighter-weight facilities for visitors.

On the first level are three glass-enclosed structures. One is a museum, the Cinemax, which shows films about the tower. The central structure comprises two levels, each of which has a restaurant. The third facility is a hall that provides space for business conferences, expositions, cultural events, and social gatherings.

On the smaller second level, there is a souvenir shop and a snack bar. From this level, it is possible to get an excellent view of Paris without the need to ascend to the top.

Reading Time _____

Recalling Facts

1. The Eiffel Tower was built as a symbol of
   - ❏ a. the French government.
   - ❏ b. World War I.
   - ❏ c. the 100th anniversary of the French Revolution.

2. For thirty years after it was built, the Eiffel Tower was
   - ❏ a. the world's tallest building.
   - ❏ b. the world's heaviest building.
   - ❏ c. in danger of collapsing.

3. The designer of the Eiffel Tower was
   - ❏ a. a noted bridge engineer.
   - ❏ b. a government official.
   - ❏ c. a famous architect.

4. The Eiffel Tower was named for
   - ❏ a. the president of France.
   - ❏ b. a French historian.
   - ❏ c. its designer.

5. After it was built, the Eiffel Tower was redesigned to accommodate
   - ❏ a. a public firm's offices.
   - ❏ b. a meteorological station.
   - ❏ c. a train station.

Understanding Ideas

6. When it was built, the Eiffel Tower was
   - ❏ a. similar to other buildings in Paris.
   - ❏ b. like no other building in the world.
   - ❏ c. an extravagant and useless building.

7. After it was built, the Eiffel Tower was regarded
   - ❏ a. with mixed emotions.
   - ❏ b. as a great achievement.
   - ❏ c. with amusement.

8. It is likely that if the tower had not been made useful, it would have been
   - ❏ a. sold to the highest builder.
   - ❏ b. torn down.
   - ❏ c. closed.

9. Eiffel's tower design was probably influenced
   - ❏ a. solely by artistic considerations.
   - ❏ b. by public requests.
   - ❏ c. by his background in bridge design.

10. You can conclude from the article that today the Eiffel Tower is
    - ❏ a. no more than a symbol of the past.
    - ❏ b. the oldest building in Paris.
    - ❏ c. a popular attraction.

The Man Who Built the Eiffel Tower

Alexandre-Gustave Eiffel was born in 1832 and studied engineering in Paris. At the age of 26, he built an iron railway bridge across a river, a massive project that predicted his later career. In 1867, Eiffel established his own engineering firm, specializing in large iron works. Eiffel's designs were both elegant and strong, and he soon became well-known all over Europe.

In 1884, Eiffel designed the iron framework for the Statue of Liberty of sculptor Frédéric Auguste Bartholdi. At that time, too, the French government was planning a major exposition to celebrate the 100th anniversary of the French Revolution. The government officials turned to Eiffel to design and produce a fitting monument. The result was the Eiffel Tower.

Eiffel planned his masterpiece on paper down to the last rivet—over 12,000 metal parts and 2.5 million rivets in all. The pieces were cut and fitted together, and the prefabricated parts transported to the site where they were finally assembled. Eiffel drew on his extensive experience in constructing railway bridges high over rocky rivers to plan the construction.

Eiffel lived to be 91 years old. At the end of his life, ever the engineer, he was studying the science of aerodynamics, or how airplanes fly.

1. Recognizing Words in Context

Find the word *fitting* in the passage. One definition below is a *synonym* for that word; it means the same or almost the same thing. One definition is an *antonym;* it has the opposite or nearly opposite meaning. The other has a completely different meaning. Label the definitions S for *synonym,* A for *antonym,* and D for *different.*

_____ a. improper

_____ b. suitable

_____ c. equipping

2. Distinguishing Fact from Opinion

Two of the statements below present *facts,* which can be proved correct. The other statement is an *opinion,* which expresses someone's thoughts or beliefs. Label the statements F for *fact* and O for *opinion.*

_____ a. Eiffel designed the framework for the Statue of Liberty.

_____ b. The Eiffel Tower had 12,000 metal parts and over two million rivets.

_____ c. Eiffel's designs were both elegant and strong.

3. Keeping Events in Order

Label the statements below 1, 2, and 3 to show the order in which the events happened.

_____ a. Eiffel set up his own engineering firm.

_____ b. Eiffel planned the Eiffel Tower on paper.

_____ c. Eiffel built his first iron railway bridge.

4. Making Correct Inferences

Two of the statements below are correct *inferences*, or reasonable guesses. They are based on information in the passage. The other statement is an incorrect, or faulty, inference. Label the statements C for *correct* inference and F for *faulty* inference.

_____ a. The Eiffel Tower made Eiffel famous.

_____ b. Eiffel was a gifted engineer.

_____ c. Eiffel's attention to detail was enormous.

5. Understanding Main Ideas

One of the statements below expresses the main idea of the passage. One statement is too general, or too broad. The other explains only part of the passage; it is too narrow. Label the statements M for *main idea*, B for *too broad*, and N for *too narrow*.

_____ a. Alexandre-Gustave Eiffel was a famous French engineer.

_____ b. Eiffel planned the Eiffel Tower on paper down to the last rivet, fitted the pieces together, and transported them to the site where they were finally assembled.

_____ c. Alexandre-Gustave Eiffel had a distinguished career in engineering that included many projects such as the Statue of Liberty and the Eiffel Tower.

Correct Answers, Part A _____

Correct Answers, Part B _____

Total Correct Answers _____

15   A   The Partnership of Dog and Human

Authorities agree that the dog was the first animal domesticated by humans. How and when this domestication took place, however, remains unknown. A 50,000-year-old cave painting in Europe seems to show a doglike animal hunting with people. But most experts believe the dog was domesticated only within the last 15,000 years.

One theory holds that humans took wolf pups back to their camp or cave, reared the pups, and allowed the tame wolves to hunt with them. Later they accepted pups of the tame wolves into the family circle. Another theory suggests that dogs were attracted to food scraps dumped as waste near human living sites, and as they scavenged and kept the site clean, the dogs rendered a service to the humans. In turn, the humans learned to accept the presence of the scavengers. Still other theories maintain that the dog was domesticated to pull sleds and other conveyances bearing the heavy game killed by humans.

Studies of primitive human societies still in existence tend to substantiate some of these theories. Whatever the ultimate reason for the dog's domestication, however, the final submission of the animal must have been the consequence of the dog's caution over thousands of years. Also, the dog, itself a hunter, had to suppress its desire to kill the other animals domesticated by humans and instead to serve as their protectors.

The partnership between dog and humans has long been shown in paintings and other art forms as well as in writings. Prehistoric paintings drawn on the walls of Spanish caves about 15,000 years ago show doglike animals accompanying humans on a hunt. Too, dogs are amply illustrated in the sculptures and pottery of such ancient civilizations as Assyria, Egypt, and Greece.

Throughout the years, dogs have been bred for many reasons, such as for hunting, herding, and guarding. Breed histories and pedigrees, however, were not methodically compiled until the establishment of the first kennel clubs in the nineteenth century. Today's breeds are a standardization of the desirable traits, especially those characteristics that have proved useful over the centuries of the older breeds. Dog breeders try to perpetuate those traits while maintaining a friendly disposition in a dog, a trait so vitally important for an animal kept as a family pet.

People have been amply repaid for this long partnership and rapport with the dog. Care and love have been exchanged for loyalty, companionship, and fun.

Reading Time _____

Recalling Facts

1. The dog was probably domesticated
   - ❑ a. 50,000 years ago.
   - ❑ b. 15,000 years ago.
   - ❑ c. in the nineteenth century.

2. One theory of how dogs became domesticated suggests that dogs descended from
   - ❑ a. wolves.
   - ❑ b. tigers.
   - ❑ c. deer.

3. Prehistoric paintings of humans and dogs hunting were discovered in caves in
   - ❑ a. Egypt.
   - ❑ b. Spain.
   - ❑ c. Canada.

4. Breed histories and pedigrees were methodically compiled when
   - ❑ a. dogs were first bred.
   - ❑ b. dogs became domesticated.
   - ❑ c. kennel clubs were established.

5. Dog breeders try to
   - ❑ a. train dogs to be good hunters.
   - ❑ b. perpetuate desirable traits in a breed.
   - ❑ c. establish new dog breeds.

Understanding Ideas

6. It is likely that humans domesticated dogs because
   - ❑ a. dogs could be useful.
   - ❑ b. dogs were religious objects.
   - ❑ c. humans were afraid of dogs.

7. In order to become domesticated, dogs had to
   - ❑ a. reverse their natural instincts.
   - ❑ b. learn to hunt by instinct.
   - ❑ c. follow their instincts.

8. You can conclude from the article that different breeds of dogs have
   - ❑ a. basically the same traits.
   - ❑ b. traits specific to the breed.
   - ❑ c. descended from different types of animals.

9. You can conclude that how dogs are bred affects
   - ❑ a. what food dogs eat.
   - ❑ b. the dogs' age.
   - ❑ c. the dogs' dispositions.

10. The article suggests that the relationship between humans and dogs
    - ❑ a. is mutually beneficial.
    - ❑ b. benefits humans more than dogs.
    - ❑ c. benefits dogs more than humans.

Guardian Sheep Dogs

In the late 1970s, researchers in the United States were looking at the problem of protecting sheep from predators—usually coyotes and dogs. In studying how other countries protected their sheep, they came up with the idea of using guardian dogs. Although dogs' instincts are usually to hunt and kill sheep, the researchers identified special European breeds that did not seem to do so. They brought some of these dogs to this country, and the Livestock Dog Project began.

From the beginning, the researchers noted differences between the guardian breeds and sheep herding dogs like collies. The herders worked by chasing and snapping at sheep whereas the guardians played with the sheep and seemed almost like sheep themselves. Only when something threatened the sheep did they react like dogs and dash to the rescue.

Sheep ranchers, at first, were leery about using guardian dogs, but many who tried them reported success. One rancher who usually lost over 100 sheep to coyotes in a season lost only two.

The experiment had its problems, however. Not all dogs worked out, and not all sheep accepted the dogs. But researchers learned a great deal about another aspect of the age-old relationship of working dogs and humans.

1. Recognizing Words in Context

Find the word *leery* in the passage. One definition below is a *synonym* for that word; it means the same or almost the same thing. One definition is an *antonym*; it has the opposite or nearly opposite meaning. The other has a completely different meaning. Label the definitions S for *synonym*, A for *antonym*, and D for *different*.

_____ a. trusting

_____ b. suspicious

_____ c. joyful

2. Distinguishing Fact from Opinion

Two of the statements below present *facts*, which can be proved correct. The other statement is an *opinion*, which expresses someone's thoughts or beliefs. Label the statements F for *fact* and O for *opinion*.

_____ a. The guardian dogs seemed almost like sheep themselves.

_____ b. Dogs' instincts are usually to hunt and kill sheep.

_____ c. One rancher who usually lost 100 sheep lost only two.

3. Keeping Events in Order

Label the statements below 1, 2, and 3 to show the order in which the events happened.

_____ a. Researchers brought guardian breeds of dogs to this country.

_____ b. Researchers noted that guardian and herder dogs worked differently.

_____ c. Ranchers who tried the dogs reported success.

4. Making Correct Inferences

Two of the statements below are correct *inferences*, or reasonable guesses. They are based on information in the passage. The other statement is an incorrect, or faulty, inference. Label the statements C for *correct* inference and F for *faulty* inference.

_____ a. Guardian sheep dogs have been bred to reduce some instinctive behaviors.

_____ b. Dogs cannot be trusted around sheep.

_____ c. If more ranchers used guardian dogs, losses could be reduced.

5. Understanding Main Ideas

One of the statements below expresses the main idea of the passage. One statement is too general, or too broad. The other explains only part of the passage; it is too narrow. Label the statements M for *main idea*, B for *too broad*, and N for *too narrow*.

_____ a. Sheep dogs can guard sheep.

_____ b. From the beginning, researchers noted that herders worked by chasing sheep, and guardians reacted only when something threatened the sheep.

_____ c. Although dogs usually harm sheep, researchers found that certain breeds make successful guardians and can reduce losses to predators.

Correct Answers, Part A _____

Correct Answers, Part B _____

Total Correct Answers _____

Initiative, Referendum, and Recall

Taken together, initiative, referendum, and recall are the politics of direct action. These three processes are means by which the people may bring their will to bear directly on the legislative process and the machinery of government. Most constitutional democracies, such as those in Australia, Canada, and the United States, operate through a system of representative government. When the people are dissatisfied with and want to change the actions of government or when the government wants to get public approval for a policy, these three devices are available.

Initiative is a legislative proposal that originates with the people. By recall, voters may initiate a process to remove public officials from office. Referendum, however, is a measure the government submits to the people for their approval. All three have in common the fact that, at some point or another, the people vote on them.

Through initiative, any proposed law can be put on the ballot in an election. To use initiative, citizens must gather petitions signed by a certain portion of voters. If the petitions are approved and the signatures are valid, the proposal can be voted on. If it passes, the proposal becomes law. Sometimes initiatives are first submitted to a legislature. If they are passed in the legislature, they become laws without the need for a popular vote. If they fail, they may be submitted directly to a vote by the public, who may override the action of the legislature.

There are two kinds of referenda: obligatory and optional. In many areas, certain proposals must be put on the ballot for public approval. For example, when a school district wants to issue bonds for building new schools, it goes to the voters with an obligatory referendum. In the United States, amendments to state constitutions also must be put before the voters for approval.

Under the optional referendum, a specified number of voters may, by petition, demand a popular vote on a law passed by the legislature. By this means, an act of the legislature can be overturned in a kind of popular veto.

Recall is a device, used mostly in the United States at the state and local level, whereby voters may remove a public official from office before the expiration of his or her term. It is based on the principle that officeholders are agents of the popular will and should, therefore, be constantly subject to the public's control.

Reading Time _____

Recalling Facts

1. Initiative, referendum, and recall can be used by people to
   - ❏ a. change the actions of a government.
   - ❏ b. run for public office.
   - ❏ c. influence jury decisions.

2. Of the three politics of direct action, the two that originate with the people are
   - ❏ a. initiative and referendum.
   - ❏ b. referendum and recall.
   - ❏ c. initiative and recall.

3. Any proposed law can be put on the ballot in an election through
   - ❏ a. recall.
   - ❏ b. initiative.
   - ❏ c. referendum.

4. When a school district wants to issue bonds for construction, it goes to the public with
   - ❏ a. an initiative.
   - ❏ b. a constitutional amendment.
   - ❏ c. an obligatory referendum.

5. The device based on the principle that officeholders are subject to the control of the voters is
   - ❏ a. optional referendum.
   - ❏ b. recall.
   - ❏ c. obligation.

Understanding Ideas

6. Initiative, referendum, and recall are based on the concept that
   - ❏ a. government is subject to the will of the people.
   - ❏ b. politics is best left to elected officials.
   - ❏ c. voters should become more involved in government policy.

7. You can conclude from the article that in a country that lacks a representative government,
   - ❏ a. people are not dissatisfied with their government.
   - ❏ b. government policy is decided by the people.
   - ❏ c. people cannot act to change government policy.

8. It is unlikely that recall could be used
   - ❏ a. to remove the president of the United States from office.
   - ❏ b. to remove a state official from office.
   - ❏ c. at the local level.

9. The politics of direct action assume that
   - ❏ a. laws are unreliable.
   - ❏ b. the needs of people may change.
   - ❏ c. public officials are corrupt.

10. You can conclude that in most states, a state constitutional amendment
    - ❏ a. cannot be signed by the state's governor.
    - ❏ b. requires only the legislature's approval.
    - ❏ c. must be submitted to the voters by referendum for approval.

Our old library was bursting at the seams, with no room for new materials and technology, no handicapped access, and inadequate parking. The town council agreed to put on the ballot a bond issue to expand the library, but we were worried. The town had voted down bond issues in the past; nobody wanted to pay more taxes.

Librarians began speaking to library volunteers, regular patrons, and staff members, asking them to help. At the same time, they also contacted community leaders. The group they formed—Friends of the Library—provided funds to start a publicity campaign. The Friends held book sales and visited schools to increase library membership.

Volunteers got lists of voters and looked up their addresses and telephone numbers. They put together a newsletter about the library and sent a copy to every registered voter. They set up information tables in the library and other public places and passed out "Vote Yes" buttons. The day of the election, volunteers called registered voters, urging them to vote "yes."

The referendum passed by a wide margin. Library management, staff, and volunteers all breathed a sigh of relief. We learned a lot about the political process, and our town will now have a modern, expanded library for the future.

1. Recognizing Words in Context

Find the word *expand* in the passage. One definition below is a *synonym* for that word; it means the same or almost the same thing. One definition is an *antonym;* it has the opposite or nearly opposite meaning. The other has a completely different meaning. Label the definitions S for *synonym*, A for *antonym*, and D for *different*.

_____ a. stretch

_____ b. contract

_____ c. enlarge

2. Distinguishing Fact from Opinion

Two of the statements below present *facts,* which can be proved correct. The other statement is an *opinion,* which expresses someone's thoughts or beliefs. Label the statements F for *fact* and O for *opinion*.

_____ a. The library had no handicapped access.

_____ b. The referendum passed.

_____ c. It would not be fair to ask people to pay higher taxes for a new library.

3. Keeping Events in Order

Two of the statements below describe events that happened at the same time. The other statement describes an event that happened before or after those events. Label them S for *same time,* B for *before,* and A for *after.*

_____ a. They formed a group called Friends of the Library.

_____ b. Librarians spoke to library volunteers, regular patrons, and staff members.

_____ c. Librarians contacted community leaders.

4. Making Correct Inferences

Two of the statements below are correct *inferences,* or reasonable guesses. They are based on information in the passage. The other statement is an incorrect, or faulty, inference. Label the statements C for *correct* inference and F for *faulty* inference.

_____ a. The success of the referendum depended on volunteer help.

_____ b. The referendum would have passed without the publicity campaign.

_____ c. The library needed to be expanded.

5. Understanding Main Ideas

One of the statements below expresses the main idea of the passage. One statement is too general, or too broad. The other explains only part of the passage; it is too narrow. Label the statements M for *main idea,* B for *too broad,* and N for *too narrow.*

_____ a. Library management and staff, community leaders, and volunteers worked together to get voters to pass a library referendum.

_____ b. A referendum is a measure submitted by the government to the people for their approval.

_____ c. Volunteers got lists of voters, sent them a newsletter, and later called, asking them to vote "yes."

Correct Answers, Part A _____

Correct Answers, Part B _____

Total Correct Answers _____

The Warrior Huns

During the third century B.C., China began to reinforce parts of the Great Wall of China in hopes that the wall would help keep out a ferocious nomadic people from Mongolia to the north. The Huns, as the nomads were known in the West, were animal herders who were proficient horse riders. Over time, the Huns worked their way westward across the grasslands of Central Asia, and by about A.D. 370, they appeared in southeastern Europe. There and in Central Europe, they began assembling an immense empire.

By 376, the Huns had attacked and conquered the Visigoths on the western shores of the Black Sea in what is now Romania. For 50 years after they conquered the Visigoths, the Huns remained a chronic irritant to the Western and Eastern Roman Empires. They eventually established themselves in Europe and made incursions into the Roman provinces along the Danube River. Early in the fifth century, they apparently extended their authority over Germanic peoples to the west.

The Huns were outstanding warriors whose accomplishments as mounted archers astonished the Romans and caused great apprehension throughout Europe. For most of their history, the Huns were governed by chieftains, but this situation changed in the fifth century. By 432, the leadership of the Huns had become centralized under a capable ruler King Rugila. After the king died in 434, he was succeeded by his two sons, Bleda and Attila. The two shared authority until Attila assassinated Bleda and took sole control of the empire in 445.

Attila was a resolute and autocratic ruler who administered his vast empire through a group of emissaries, or representatives. The emissaries discharged diplomatic missions, served as commanders of military campaigns, and collected tribute from subject peoples.

It was the long-suffering conquered peoples who ultimately destroyed the Huns' empire. First, Attila suffered a huge military defeat in France and later was driven from Italy by a plague in 452. He died the following year and was succeeded by his many sons, who fought constantly among themselves. The subject peoples of the empire took the opportunity to rebel and overthrow the Huns.

The Huns were decisively defeated in 455. The former Byzantine Empire reclaimed its frontiers and suspended trade relations with the Huns. Sporadic raids by some of Attila's sons continued for a few years, but by the end of the century, the Huns had disintegrated as a separate people.

Reading Time _____

Recalling Facts

1. The Huns were known as outstanding
   - ❏ a. warriors.
   - ❏ b. farmers.
   - ❏ c. artists.

2. For most of their history, the Huns were governed by
   - ❏ a. religious leaders.
   - ❏ b. foreign rulers.
   - ❏ c. chieftains.

3. A Hun leader who gained sole control of the Huns' empire by assassinating his brother was
   - ❏ a. Rugila.
   - ❏ b. Attila.
   - ❏ c. Bleda.

4. The Huns originated in
   - ❏ a. Mongolia.
   - ❏ b. Germany.
   - ❏ c. Rome.

5. Attila was driven from Italy in 452 by
   - ❏ a. Roman forces.
   - ❏ b. rebelling subject peoples.
   - ❏ c. a plague.

Understanding Ideas

6. The Huns could be described as
   - ❏ a. fearsome.
   - ❏ b. peace-loving.
   - ❏ c. isolationists.

7. You can conclude from the article that historically empires tend to
   - ❏ a. self-destruct.
   - ❏ b. peak and then wane in power.
   - ❏ c. sustain power for many centuries.

8. Groups like the Huns assumed power by
   - ❏ a. beating enemies in debates.
   - ❏ b. conquering other groups in battle.
   - ❏ c. exerting religious authority.

9. You can conclude that prior to the rule of King Rugila, the Huns were essentially
   - ❏ a. a close-knit group of people.
   - ❏ b. peaceful animal herders.
   - ❏ c. widely dispersed nomads.

10. Probably the Huns' greatest assets were
    - ❏ a. scholarship and a love of animals.
    - ❏ b. horse riding and fighting abilities.
    - ❏ c. democratic government and peacekeeping.

17 | B — The Battle of Châlons

In A.D. 451, Attila, "the Scourge of God," swept across the Rhine River with 40,000 Hun warriors, invaded Gaul, and conquered the city of Orléans. The Roman military commander, Flavius Aëtius, quickly joined with Theodoric I, king of the Visigoths, to battle the Huns. Attila was forced to retreat from Orléans with the Roman-Visigothic army in pursuit.

Near Châlons, Attila halted his retreat and swung his army around to face his enemies. Aëtius and the Roman legions waited on a hill on the west flank as a force of Alan tribal fighters stood in the center, and the Visigoths guarded the east flank.

Attila began the battle by launching an assault on the Romans, who repeatedly threw his forces back. The Huns, however, succeeded in pushing back the Alans. To counter this, Theodoric attacked the Huns from the east. Struck by a javelin, Theodoric fell from his horse and was trampled to death by his own charging warriors. His son, Thorismond, took command, and the Visigoths, enraged by their king's death, fell on the Huns in a fury. The Huns were forced to fall back to their camp.

Aëtius allowed the Huns to retreat back across the Rhine the next day. Attila had experienced his first and only defeat.

1. **Recognizing Words in Context**

Find the word *face* in the passage. One definition below is a *synonym* for that word; it means the same or almost the same thing. One definition is an *antonym*; it has the opposite or nearly opposite meaning. The other has a completely different meaning. Label the definitions S for *synonym*, A for *antonym*, and D for *different*.

_____ a. avoid

_____ b. countenance

_____ c. confront

2. **Distinguishing Fact from Opinion**

Two of the statements below present *facts*, which can be proved correct. The other statement is an *opinion*, which expresses someone's thoughts or beliefs. Label the statements F for *fact* and O for *opinion*.

_____ a. Attila invaded Gaul with 40,000 Hun warriors in A.D. 451.

_____ b. Attila was foolish to try to fight the Romans and Visigoths.

_____ c. The Romans and Visigoths joined forces to battle the Huns.

3. Keeping Events in Order

Two of the statements below describe events that happened at the same time. The other statement describes an event that happened before or after those events. Label them S for *same time,* B for *before,* and A for *after.*

_____ a. The Huns succeeded in pushing back the Alans.

_____ b. The Huns fell back to their camp.

_____ c. The Visigoths attacked the Huns from the east.

4. Making Correct Inferences

Two of the statements below are correct *inferences,* or reasonable guesses. They are based on information in the passage. The other statement is an incorrect, or faulty, inference. Label the statements C for *correct* inference and F for *faulty* inference.

_____ a. Attila had not expected to suffer a defeat in Gaul.

_____ b. Attila learned a lesson from his defeat in Gaul.

_____ c. The joined Roman-Visigothic forces were superior to the Huns.

5. Understanding Main Ideas

One of the statements below expresses the main idea of the passage. One statement is too general, or too broad. The other explains only part of the passage; it is too narrow. Label the statements M for *main idea,* B for *too broad,* and N for *too narrow.*

_____ a. Attila was king of the Huns from A.D. 434 to 453.

_____ b. Attila's first conquest in Gaul was the city of Orléans.

_____ c. Attila, leader of the Huns, suffered his first and only defeat at the battle of Châlons in A.D. 451.

Correct Answers, Part A _____

Correct Answers, Part B _____

Total Correct Answers _____

| 18 | A | The Insect World

The world's most abundant creatures are the insects, and the known species of insects outnumber all the other animals and the plants combined. Insects have been so successful in their fight for life that they are sometimes described as the human race's closest rivals for domination of the earth. Small size, relatively minimal food requirements, and rapid reproduction have all helped perpetuate the many species of insects. Entomologists, scientists who study insects, have named almost 1,000,000 species—perhaps less than one-third of the total number.

Insects thrive in almost any habitat where life is possible. Some are found only in the Arctic regions, and some live only in deserts. Others thrive only in fresh water or only in brackish water. Many species of insects are able to tolerate both freezing and tropical temperatures. Such hardy species are often found to range widely over the earth. Few insects, however, inhabit marine environments.

Certain parasitic insects spend much of their lives on or within the body of an animal host where all the necessities of life, such as food, moisture, warmth, and protection from enemies, are optimal. Other kinds of insects spend all or some part of their lives securely enclosed in a food plant.

Some species have become remarkably versatile as they adapt in order to meet the changing demands of the environment. Various water bugs and water beetles, for example, are able to fly and swim as well as crawl. Many types of insects, such as the bees, ants, and wasps, depend on a complex social structure and defensive behavior. Nonpredatory species frequently have defenses such as an unpleasant taste or odor, venomous spines, and camouflage that help protect them from enemies.

Although they are adaptable and versatile as a group, insects are often unable to adjust to weather extremes such as excessive rain, early frost, and extended drought that can quickly wipe out or drastically reduce insect populations in a region. Because insects are an important part of the diet of many animals—birds, reptiles, amphibians, and fish, as well as other insects—the number is constantly held in check.

The number of factors unfavorable to the survival of individual insects is overwhelming. As a result, in some species, only a few individuals out of hundreds of eggs laid by a single female reach adulthood. The survival of some species is enhanced by the large numbers of eggs laid.

Reading Time _____

Recalling Facts

1. Entomologists are scientists who study
   - ❑ a. habitats.
   - ❑ b. parasites.
   - ❑ c. insects.

2. Insects thrive
   - ❑ a. in almost any habitat where life is possible.
   - ❑ b. primarily in colder habitats.
   - ❑ c. primarily in warmer habitats.

3. Fewer insects are found in
   - ❑ a. fresh water.
   - ❑ b. brackish water.
   - ❑ c. marine environments.

4. Insects that live on or within the body of an animal host are
   - ❑ a. social insects.
   - ❑ b. parasites.
   - ❑ c. water dwellers.

5. To enhance survival, insects
   - ❑ a. avoid extreme environmental conditions.
   - ❑ b. lay large numbers of eggs.
   - ❑ c. migrate constantly.

Understanding Ideas

6. An insect's small size is an advantage because
   - ❑ a. it can develop defenses.
   - ❑ b. it can better tolerate tropical temperatures.
   - ❑ c. it can easily hide from predators.

7. The insect's greatest advantage is probably
   - ❑ a. abundance.
   - ❑ b. adaptability.
   - ❑ c. minor food requirements.

8. Humans should probably regard insects
   - ❑ a. as dangerous rivals.
   - ❑ b. with respect.
   - ❑ c. with contempt.

9. You can conclude from the article that insects outnumber other animals because
   - ❑ a. they are smarter.
   - ❑ b. more species have been named.
   - ❑ c. they have developed better survival skills.

10. The number of known insect species will most likely
    - ❑ a. continue to grow.
    - ❑ b. decrease.
    - ❑ c. stay the same.

The Body Snatchers

A scout emerges from her underground dwelling and wanders across the hot Arizona desert, searching for signs of life. Suddenly she spies what she is looking for—a busy colony with thousands of inhabitants. The scout carefully marks the colony's position and hurriedly returns to her home base to alert the others.

Within minutes an army of 3,000 invaders, led by the scout, advances steadfastly across the desert floor. When they reach the unsuspecting colony, the marauders spray a macelike chemical into the openings of the underground chambers. The attacked queen and her workers flee their chambers in panic, leaving behind their young that are not old enough to fend for themselves.

It is just these young that the raiders are after. Each invader snatches up one of the young and carries it back to the attackers' home. There the raiders will raise the captured youngsters to serve as slaves. When they are grown, they will gather food, feed the young of their new queen, and maintain the nest. They will do all this willingly, believing that they belong to the raiders' colony. They were captured so young that they will not have any knowledge of another home. To them, their captors are family. Without such slaves, the raiders—western slave-making ants, *Polyergus breviceps*—are so helpless they would die.

1. Recognizing Words in Context

Find the word *knowledge* in the passage. One definition below is a *synonym* for that word; it means the same or almost the same thing. One definition is an *antonym;* it has the opposite or nearly opposite meaning. The other has a completely different meaning. Label the definitions S for *synonym,* A for *antonym,* and D for *different.*

_____ a. memory

_____ b. forgetfulness

_____ c. learning

2. Distinguishing Fact from Opinion

Two of the statements below present *facts,* which can be proved correct. The other statement is an *opinion,* which expresses someone's thoughts or beliefs. Label the statements F for *fact* and O for *opinion.*

_____ a. These ants have developed an amazing lifestyle.

_____ b. The invading ants captured the other ants' young and carried them off to serve as slaves.

_____ c. The young ants will serve as their captors' slaves.

3. Keeping Events in Order

Two of the statements below describe events that happened at the same time. The other statement describes an event that happened before or after those events. Label them S for *same time,* B for *before,* and A for *after.*

_____ a. The attacked queen and her workers flee their nest.

_____ b. The raiders spray a macelike chemical into the nest.

_____ c. The young are left behind in the nest.

4. Making Correct Inferences

Two of the statements below are correct *inferences,* or reasonable guesses. They are based on information in the passage. The other statement is an incorrect, or faulty, inference. Label the statements C for *correct* inference and F for *faulty* inference.

_____ a. The attacking ants need a constant supply of young ants to maintain their colony.

_____ b. The slave-making ants have a very easy life.

_____ c. The ant slaves are not aware that they have been enslaved.

5. Understanding Main Ideas

One of the statements below expresses the main idea of the passage. One statement is too general, or too broad. The other explains only part of the passage; it is too narrow. Label the statements M for *main idea,* B for *too broad,* and N for *too narrow.*

_____ a. Each raider snatches up one of the young and carries it back home.

_____ b. The western slave-making ant captures the young of other ants to work as slaves.

_____ c. The many different kinds of ants in the world have developed some unusual survival methods.

Correct Answers, Part A _____

Correct Answers, Part B _____

Total Correct Answers _____

A Brilliant Pianist

The most brilliant pianist of his day, Franz Liszt was also a distinguished composer of great originality and a major figure in Romantic music. Liszt was born on October 22, 1811, in Raiding, Hungary, where his father was employed by the Esterhazy family as a steward and was himself an amateur musician. The Esterhazy family had distinguished themselves as enthusiastic patrons of music for many generations.

Liszt's father taught him to play the piano, and at the age of 9, Liszt gave concerts at Sopron and Pozsony and at Prince Nicolas Esterhazy's palace. Liszt went to Vienna, where he studied with two well-known teachers, Carl Czerny and Antonio Salieri. He gave his first public concerts in Vienna in 1822 and in Paris and London in 1824. His playing moved Beethoven to kiss him, and in England, King George IV received him at Windsor. In Paris, where he lived for 12 years, he was sensationally successful.

In 1835, Liszt was joined in Geneva by the Countess Marie d'Agoult, with whom he had a daughter, Cosima, who became the wife of the conductor Hans von Bulow and then of the composer Richard Wagner. Triumphant concert tours dominated Liszt's life until September 1847, when he made his last appearance as a virtuoso.

From 1848 to 1859, he conducted at the court and theater at Weimar. There he championed Wagner's music and produced Wagner's musical dramas. Liszt also introduced and revived the works of other contemporary composers. During these years, his most productive period, he composed 12 symphonic poems, the *Faust* and *Dante* symphonies, the piano sonata, two piano concertos, and *Totentanz* for piano and orchestra. It was also during this period that he revised versions of the Paganini Etudes and the Transcendental Etudes.

At 50, Liszt retired to Rome where he received minor orders in the Roman Catholic Church. In Rome, he was occupied with religious music, composing two oratorios and a number of smaller works. He again began visiting Weimar regularly, and the Hungarian government named him president of the Academy of Music at Budapest. Thereafter he divided his time among Rome, Weimar, and Budapest. His last works were harmonically very advanced, anticipating musical forms of the twentieth century. These works were, however, long neglected. After a highly spectacular jubilee tour to Paris, London, and other cities in 1886, he died at Bayreuth, in western Germany, of pneumonia on July 31.

Reading Time _____

Recalling Facts

1. Franz Liszt was born in
   - ❏ a. Paris, France.
   - ❏ b. Rome, Italy.
   - ❏ c. Raiding, Hungary.

2. Liszt learned to play the piano
   - ❏ a. at a late age.
   - ❏ b. from his father.
   - ❏ c. without any training.

3. Liszt championed the music of
   - ❏ a. Wagner.
   - ❏ b. George IV.
   - ❏ c. Beethoven.

4. The Hungarian government named Liszt president of the Academy of Music in
   - ❏ a. Rome.
   - ❏ b. Budapest.
   - ❏ c. Weimar.

5. Liszt's most productive period was
   - ❏ a. as a traveling musician.
   - ❏ b. after his last virtuoso performance.
   - ❏ c. during his youth.

Understanding Ideas

6. You can conclude from the article that Liszt was considered
   - ❏ a. a well-rounded musician.
   - ❏ b. a better musician than composer.
   - ❏ c. a brilliant violinist.

7. Liszt supported the works of contemporary composers, which suggests that
   - ❏ a. Liszt was jealous of other musicians.
   - ❏ b. Liszt was a generous person.
   - ❏ c. Liszt could no longer write music himself.

8. You can conclude from the article that Liszt retired as a piano virtuoso
   - ❏ a. because he could no longer play well.
   - ❏ b. to devote more time to composing.
   - ❏ c. to learn to play the violin.

9. Liszt's last works were long neglected, which suggests that
   - ❏ a. his earlier compositions were musically superior.
   - ❏ b. people of the time did not appreciate good music.
   - ❏ c. they were ahead of their time.

10. The article wants you to understand that Liszt's musical works
    - ❏ a. have never been equaled.
    - ❏ b. were appreciated only during his lifetime.
    - ❏ c. are much admired today.

Even as a young child, Franz Liszt could sight-read any piece of music put in front of him. By the time he was 12 years old, he was giving concerts and pleasing audiences all over Europe.

When Liszt was 15 years old, his father died; and for a time, young Liszt felt lost, both personally and artistically. Then at the age of 20, inspired by the example of the violinist Niccolo Paganini, Liszt hurled himself into practicing, determined to become the greatest pianist of his day.

He spent his twenties touring Europe, giving concerts that electrified audiences. Tall and strong, he left a trail of demolished pianos with snapped strings and splintered wood behind him. He began composing music so complex that few pianists could play it. Liszt's hands were huge; most of his 1,300 compositions cannot be played by people whose hands are of ordinary proportions.

When he was 35 years old, Liszt renounced solo piano work to take a position as a conductor, and never again did he play the piano in public. In the last years of his life, he welcomed a new generation of pianists to his studio, where he alternately enthralled and terrorized them until his death at the age of 75.

1. **Recognizing Words in Context**

Find the word *demolished* in the passage. One definition below is a *synonym* for that word; it means the same or almost the same thing. One definition is an *antonym*; it has the opposite or nearly opposite meaning. The other has a completely different meaning. Label the definitions S for *synonym*, A for *antonym*, and D for *different*.

_____ a. restored

_____ b. demonstrated

_____ c. destroyed

2. **Distinguishing Fact from Opinion**

Two of the statements below present *facts*, which can be proved correct. The other statement is an *opinion*, which expresses someone's thoughts or beliefs. Label the statements F for *fact* and O for *opinion*.

_____ a. Liszt was giving concerts all over Europe at the age of twelve.

_____ b. Liszt gave up solo piano playing at thirty-five.

_____ c. Liszt's concerts electrified his audiences.

3. Keeping Events in Order

Label the statements below 1, 2, and 3 to show the order in which the events happened.

_____ a. Liszt was inspired by violinist Niccolo Paganini's example.

_____ b. Liszt's father died.

_____ c. Liszt composed music so complex that few could play it.

4. Making Correct Inferences

Two of the statements below are correct *inferences*, or reasonable guesses. They are based on information in the passage. The other statement is an incorrect, or faulty, inference. Label the statements C for *correct* inference and F for *faulty* inference.

_____ a. Liszt's talent surfaced very early in his life.

_____ b. Liszt was an exceptionally good teacher.

_____ c. Liszt was a remarkable pianist.

5. Understanding Main Ideas

One of the statements below expresses the main idea of the passage. One statement is too general, or too broad. The other explains only part of the passage; it is too narrow. Label the statements M for *main idea*, B for *too broad*, and N for *too narrow*.

_____ a. As a composer, Liszt wrote pieces that only he could play.

_____ b. Franz Liszt was a great pianist.

_____ c. Franz Liszt's entire life was dedicated to his music.

Correct Answers, Part A _____

Correct Answers, Part B _____

Total Correct Answers _____

The Academy

Before the time of Plato, ambitious young Greeks in Athens depended on the Sophists for their higher education. The Sophists were traveling lecturers who provided instruction in oratory and philosophy. They were always sure to find an audience in one of the three great public gymnasiums near Athens where young men trained for athletic contests.

When Plato returned to Athens from his travels in about 387 B.C., he settled in a house near a gymnasium called the Academy, about a mile (1.6 kilometers) northwest of the city walls. He organized a college with a definite membership, which met sometimes within the walls of the Academy and sometimes in his own house or garden. Other philosophers followed his example in choosing a fixed place for their lectures and discussions. Aristotle, a pupil of Plato, set up his school in the Lyceum, a gymnasium east of the city.

The names associated with these Greek schools and discussion groups have been carried down to present times with a wide variety of meanings. The Germans, for example, use the word *gymnasium* not for a place for athletic exercises but for a secondary school. In France, a *lycee* is a secondary school. In the United States, *lyceum* once meant a group that met for lectures and discussion. Today it refers to a program of planned lectures and concerts.

The word *academy* is used in England and the United States for many private secondary schools and for institutions where specialized training is provided, such as riding academies and military and naval academies. The term *academy* is used in a more general way in several languages for learned societies formed to promote knowledge and culture or to advance some particular art or science.

Of these learned societies, the most famous is the French Academy, an association of literary people established in 1635. Four years later, its members began work on a dictionary. Since new words had to be approved by them before being accepted as good usage, the academicians exercised careful control over the French language. On the death of an academician, the remaining members would elect a replacement. Election to this group of scholars came to be regarded as the highest honor a French writer could receive. The French Academy later associated with four other academies to form the Institute of France. The French Academy today is best known for its Ecole des Beaux-Arts.

Reading Time _____

Recalling Facts

1. The earliest teachers in ancient Athens were
   - ❑ a. academicians.
   - ❑ b. athletes.
   - ❑ c. Sophists.

2. Traveling lecturers gave instruction in
   - ❑ a. academies.
   - ❑ b. lyceums.
   - ❑ c. public gymnasiums.

3. The first college with a definite membership was established by
   - ❑ a. Sophists.
   - ❑ b. Plato.
   - ❑ c. Aristotle.

4. In the United States, the word *lyceum* refers to a
   - ❑ a. place for athletic exercises.
   - ❑ b. secondary school.
   - ❑ c. program of planned lectures and concerts.

5. The Ecole de Beaux-Arts is located in
   - ❑ a. France.
   - ❑ b. the United States.
   - ❑ c. England.

Understanding Ideas

6. The article wants you to understand that many terms and their meanings
   - ❑ a. have changed over time.
   - ❑ b. began with the Sophists.
   - ❑ c. should remain rigid.

7. You can conclude from the article that early scholars were
   - ❑ a. very interested in philosophy.
   - ❑ b. also fine athletes.
   - ❑ c. lazy students.

8. You can conclude that in France, scholarly writers are
   - ❑ a. students of Plato.
   - ❑ b. much admired.
   - ❑ c. conceited.

9. Early Sophists can be compared to today's
   - ❑ a. college students.
   - ❑ b. speakers who give lectures around the country.
   - ❑ c. news reporters.

10. From the article, you can conclude that Greek words
   - ❑ a. have been incorporated into modern language.
   - ❑ b. are rarely used today.
   - ❑ c. are the basis for most computer terminology.

20 B The Philosopher

Aristotle, the famous Greek philosopher and scientist, was born in 384 B.C. His father was a doctor, and young Aristotle learned biology and science from him. When he was 17 years old, Aristotle went to Athens to study at Plato's school, the Academy, where he learned Greek history and philosophy.

Aristotle was still quite young when he became a tutor to the 13-year-old Alexander the Great. With Alexander, Aristotle delved into both philosophy and natural science, and the tutor and pupil became close friends.

Aristotle taught at Plato's Academy for a time, but its emphasis on mathematics did not greatly interest him. He was more interested in questioning and discussing things that did not have definite answers, and he had an avid interest in nature and enjoyed studying the biology of both plants and animals.

After Plato died, Aristotle formed his own school in the Athenian Lyceum. Alexander helped him set up his library and a museum there and encouraged his collection of plants and animals. Aristotle, however, did not spend all his time studying specimens in his museum. The Lyceum was located in a lovely grove of trees; as he taught, Aristotle wandered around the grove with his students scrambling after him. He was one of the most beloved teachers of all time.

1. **Recognizing Words in Context**

Find the word *avid* in the passage. One definition below is a *synonym* for that word; it means the same or almost the same thing. One definition is an *antonym;* it has the opposite or nearly opposite meaning. The other has a completely different meaning. Label the definitions S for *synonym,* A for *antonym,* and D for *different.*

_____ a. actual

_____ b. strong

_____ c. weak

2. **Distinguishing Fact from Opinion**

Two of the statements below present *facts,* which can be proved correct. The other statement is an *opinion,* which expresses someone's thoughts or beliefs. Label the statements F for *fact* and O for *opinion.*

_____ a. Aristotle was a Greek teacher.

_____ b. Aristotle tutored Alexander the Great.

_____ c. Aristotle liked to wander among the trees.

3. Keeping Events in Order

Label the statements below 1, 2, and 3 to show the order in which the events happened.

_____ a. Aristotle founded his own school.

_____ b. Aristotle studied under Plato.

_____ c. Aristotle taught Alexander the Great.

4. Making Correct Inferences

Two of the statements below are correct *inferences*, or reasonable guesses. They are based on information in the passage. The other statement is an incorrect, or faulty, inference. Label the statements C for *correct* inference and F for *faulty* inference.

_____ a. Aristotle's students liked him.

_____ b. Aristotle's teaching methods are unknown today.

_____ c. Aristotle enjoyed natural beauty.

5. Understanding Main Ideas

One of the statements below expresses the main idea of the passage. One statement is too general, or too broad. The other explains only part of the passage; it is too narrow. Label the statements M for *main idea*, B for *too broad*, and N for *too narrow*.

_____ a. Aristotle was a Greek teacher.

_____ b. Aristotle's life was devoted to learning and to teaching others.

_____ c. Aristotle liked to walk around as he lectured.

Correct Answers, Part A _____

Correct Answers, Part B _____

Total Correct Answers _____

Commercial Fisheries

The term *fisheries* refers to the industry, or occupation, of catching, processing, and selling fish, shellfish, and other aquatic resources. It is an international industry that has become concerned not only with harvesting but also with the correct use and preservation of fish resources.

Great technical advances have been made in fish processing in the latter half of the twentieth century. Fish provide a valuable source of protein, and commercial fisheries are aware that the quality of the product must be high in order to retain and increase their share of the market. Many processing methods have been developed. Fish and fish products are available in many forms: fresh, frozen, whole, filleted, canned, dried, salted, minced, and smoked. Industrial fish such as the menhaden are processed commercially to produce fishmeal for animal and poultry feed. Fish oil, which is mainly exported to Europe for use in margarine, shortening, and cooking oil, is another product from menhaden, as is fertilizer.

Humans have always captured fish as food. In Norway, 5,000-year-old bone fishhooks, differing little from modern ones, were found at the site of a Stone Age fishing village. The rise of the Dutch as a sea power in the seventeenth century grew from their dominance of the North Sea fisheries.

As improvements and technical advances were made, the fishing industry expanded to cover most parts of the globe where fish were found in sufficient quantity to make commercial fishing profitable. With the introduction of steam-powered vessels, and later diesel-powered ones, traveling became faster and fishing trips could be longer. The use of power equipment aboard ship made it possible for sailors to handle larger nets and other equipment. Improvements in freezing methods enabled ships to make still longer trips because the seafood would not spoil. The development of factory, or mother, ships on which filleting, freezing, canning, and the manufacturing of by-products can be conducted made it possible for large fleets of fishing vessels to operate thousands of miles (kilometers) from their home ports.

The supply of fish in the world's waters was once thought to be inexhaustible. Since the turn of the twentieth century, however, fishing activities have seriously depleted a great number of fish stocks. Conservation methods that limit gear types and catches are now often applied to ensure a continual supply of fish and fish products from the vast expanse of water that is called the sea.

Reading Time _____

Recalling Facts

1. Fish provide a valuable source of
   - ❑ a. minerals.
   - ❑ b. fat.
   - ❑ c. protein.

2. Margarine, shortening, and cooking oil are made from
   - ❑ a. fish oil.
   - ❑ b. fertilizer.
   - ❑ c. filleted fish.

3. Longer trips for fishing vessels were made possible by the invention of
   - ❑ a. large sails.
   - ❑ b. diesel engines.
   - ❑ c. new fishing methods.

4. Bone fishhooks, 5,000 years old, were found in
   - ❑ a. Holland.
   - ❑ b. England.
   - ❑ c. Norway.

5. Ships on which fish processing occurs are called
   - ❑ a. mother ships.
   - ❑ b. commercial ships.
   - ❑ c. fleets.

Understanding Ideas

6. You can conclude from the article that before modern advancements, fishing vessels were forced to
   - ❑ a. stay at sea for several months.
   - ❑ b. operate close to their home ports.
   - ❑ c. depend on good weather to operate.

7. You can conclude that industrial fish
   - ❑ a. are not very useful.
   - ❑ b. make excellent eating.
   - ❑ c. are more useful for their by-products than as food.

8. A likely problem faced by early fishing vessels was
   - ❑ a. keeping fish fresh.
   - ❑ b. finding sufficient quantities of fish.
   - ❑ c. polluted seas.

9. A dwindling fish supply has resulted from
   - ❑ a. technical advances in the fishing industry.
   - ❑ b. years of bad weather.
   - ❑ c. poor fishing methods.

10. The article suggests that the world's supply of fish
   - ❑ a. will continue to dwindle.
   - ❑ b. will remain stable.
   - ❑ c. is inexhaustible.

A Fishing, We Will Go

We rose at 3:15 A.M. for a morning of deep-sea salmon fishing. Fog slowed our drive, and we arrived at the pier at 5:45 with barely enough time to purchase our fishing licenses and down motion-sickness tablets. The charter boat was leaving promptly at 6:00.

On open water, the captain cut the motor, and the boat drifted. Attendants baited our hooks and dropped the lines over the side, and then we waited and watched our poles. At first, there was very little activity, and we changed location several times. Then Bob's pole jumped. He grabbed it and started cranking the reel rapidly, but in just a matter of seconds, the line went slack. Almost immediately, Gail got a bite and everybody shouted, "Keep the line tight!" Gail struggled, making no headway against the frantic fish, so an attendant grabbed her rod and reeled the fish in. Others netted this first catch of the day and swung it onto the deck.

In three hours, everyone aboard the boat had caught at least one salmon. I caught two fairly large salmon—13 and 15 pounds (5 and 6 kilograms)— that I proudly held up as I posed for snapshots. Then the fish went to the cannery, which gave each of us an amount of canned salmon equal to what we had caught. Tired but happy, we headed home for breakfast and a long nap.

1. Recognizing Words in Context

Find the word *cut* in the passage. One definition below is a *synonym* for that word; it means the same or almost the same thing. One definition is an *antonym;* it has the opposite or nearly opposite meaning. The other has a completely different meaning. Label the definitions S for *synonym,* A for *antonym,* and D for *different.*

_____ a. stopped

_____ b. started

_____ c. sliced

2. Distinguishing Fact from Opinion

Two of the statements below present *facts,* which can be proved correct. The other statement is an *opinion,* which expresses someone's thoughts or beliefs. Label the statements F for *fact* and O for *opinion.*

_____ a. Everyone caught at least one salmon.

_____ b. The attendants should have let Gail catch her own fish.

_____ c. One salmon weighed 15 pounds (6 kilograms).

3. Keeping Events in Order

Two of the statements below describe events that happened at the same time. The other statement describes an event that happened before or after those events. Label them S for *same time*, B for *before*, and A for *after*.

_____ a. Bob started to crank the reel rapidly.

_____ b. Gail got a bite.

_____ c. Everyone shouted, "Keep the line tight!"

4. Making Correct Inferences

Two of the statements below are correct *inferences*, or reasonable guesses. They are based on information in the passage. The other statement is an incorrect, or faulty, inference. Label the statements C for *correct* inference and F for *faulty* inference.

_____ a. Successful deep-sea salmon fishing requires experience.

_____ b. In charter-boat fishing, attendants do a lot of the work.

_____ c. Anyone may catch a fish on a charter trip.

5. Understanding Main Ideas

One of the statements below expresses the main idea of the passage. One statement is too general, or too broad. The other explains only part of the passage; it is too narrow. Label the statements M for *main idea*, B for *too broad*, and N for *too narrow*.

_____ a. Gail, unable to reel in her fish, is helped by an attendant.

_____ b. Deep-sea salmon fishing, in one person's experience, includes periods of both little or no activity and high excitement.

_____ c. Deep-sea salmon fishing is a popular sport.

Correct Answers, Part A _____

Correct Answers, Part B _____

Total Correct Answers _____

In order for a chemical to be considered a drug, it must have the capacity to affect how the body works. No substance that has the power to do this is completely safe. Drugs are approved only after tests have demonstrated that they are relatively safe when used as directed and when their benefits outweigh their risks. Thus, some very dangerous drugs are approved because they are necessary to treat serious illness. For example, digitalis, which causes the heart muscle to contract, is a dangerous drug. Doctors are permitted to use it to treat patients with weak heart muscles, but digitalis would not be approved for treating such minor ailments as temporary fatigue because the risks outweigh the benefits.

Many persons suffer ill effects from drugs, called side effects, even though they take the drug exactly as directed. The human population, unlike a colony of ants, contains a great variety of genetic variation, but drugs are tested on just a few thousand people. When a particular drug is taken by millions, some people may not respond in a predictable way even though the drug has been tested. A person's unusual response to a particular sedative, for example, may be excitement rather than relaxation. Other people may suffer reactions to drugs that resemble allergies.

A patient may also acquire a tolerance for a certain drug, which means that ever-larger doses are necessary to produce the desired therapeutic effect. Tolerance may lead to habituation, in which the person becomes so dependent upon the drug that he or she becomes addicted to it. Addiction causes severe psychological and physical disturbances when the drug is taken away. Morphine, cocaine, and Benzedrine are common habit-forming drugs. Finally, drugs often have unwanted side effects. These usually cause only minor discomfort such as a skin rash, headache, or drowsiness. Certain drugs, however, can produce serious adverse reactions.

In the United States, the Food and Drug Administration (FDA) regulates the manufacture and sale of medicinal drugs. Since 1962, the law has required manufacturers to prove that their drugs are effective as well as safe; manufacturers must prove that the drugs actually work as claimed. The FDA regulates ethical, or prescription, drugs and proprietary drugs, also known as over-the-counter drugs. Ethical drugs can be obtained only with a prescription, while proprietary drugs, which generally treat only the symptoms, not the cause, of an illness, do not require a prescription.

Reading Time _____

Recalling Facts

1. Drugs are approved only when they are considered
   - ❏ a. completely harmless.
   - ❏ b. potentially dangerous.
   - ❏ c. relatively safe.

2. Drugs should be taken only when
   - ❏ a. the risks outweigh the benefits.
   - ❏ b. the benefits are guaranteed.
   - ❏ c. the benefits outweigh the risks.

3. A patient taking a drug may experience a dangerous progression from
   - ❏ a. tolerance to habituation to addiction.
   - ❏ b. habituation to tolerance to addiction.
   - ❏ c. addiction to habituation to tolerance.

4. Genetic variations in people may result in
   - ❏ a. a variety of reactions to the same drug.
   - ❏ b. predictable responses to certain drugs.
   - ❏ c. habit-forming drugs.

5. Proprietary drugs
   - ❏ a. require a prescription.
   - ❏ b. treat the cause of an illness.
   - ❏ c. treat the symptoms of an illness.

Understanding Ideas

6. People who habitually use a habit-forming drug are likely to become
   - ❏ a. physically impaired.
   - ❏ b. addicted to the drug.
   - ❏ c. allergic to the drug.

7. You can conclude from the article that the side effects of drugs
   - ❏ a. cause only minor discomfort.
   - ❏ b. vary with the individual.
   - ❏ c. are worth the risks.

8. In order for a drug to be available in the United States,
   - ❏ a. it must first be widely used in other countries.
   - ❏ b. it must meet standards set by the FDA.
   - ❏ c. it must not produce side effects in those who test the drug.

9. It is likely that without FDA regulation,
   - ❏ a. ineffective and unsafe drugs would be marketed.
   - ❏ b. drug manufacturers would limit their production.
   - ❏ c. more effective drugs would be available.

10. You can conclude that the most potentially dangerous drugs are
    - ❏ a. ethical drugs.
    - ❏ b. proprietary drugs.
    - ❏ c. nonprescription drugs.

22   B   Solving a Medical Mystery

In July 1996, Dr. Heidi Connolly, a heart doctor at Minnesota's Mayo Clinic, saw a patient with a rare heart condition in which waxy tissue coated the heart valves, preventing them from closing completely. This condition suggested some sort of drug reaction. The drugs the woman had been taking were fen/phen, the diet drugs fenfluramine and phentermine. Soon other patients with a similar heart valve problem turned up.

The U.S. Food and Drug Administration (FDA) had approved these drugs as safe. Could they be the cause? If so, the problem could be serious because more than 18 million fen/phen prescriptions were written in 1996!

Connolly suspected fen/phen was the culprit. Dr. Jack L. Crary, a North Dakota doctor, supported Connolly's finding when he discovered that 19 out of 24 of his patients on fen/phen had severe heart valve problems. In September 1997, the FDA conducted its own review and found that 30 percent of fen/phen users had potential heart valve problems. The drugs fenfluramine and dexfenfluramine—the fen of fen/phen—were withdrawn from the market. Phentermine—phen—was not withdrawn, because it has not been linked to the heart problems. Because of the dedication of Dr. Connolly and other physicians, a major health crisis was averted.

1. **Recognizing Words in Context**

   Find the word *finding* in the passage. One definition below is a *synonym* for that word; it means the same or almost the same thing. One definition is an *antonym;* it has the opposite or nearly opposite meaning. The other has a completely different meaning. Label the definitions S for *synonym,* A for *antonym,* and D for *different*.

   _____ a. attaining

   _____ b. discovery

   _____ c. concealment

2. **Distinguishing Fact from Opinion**

   Two of the statements below present *facts,* which can be proved correct. The other statement is an *opinion,* which expresses someone's thoughts or beliefs. Label the statements F for *fact* and O for *opinion.*

   _____ a. Connolly's patients were taking fen/phen.

   _____ b. The FDA should not have approved the use of fen/phen without further study.

   _____ c. Connolly's patients had a rare heart condition.

3. Keeping Events in Order

Label the statements below 1, 2, and 3 to show the order in which the events happened.

_____ a. The fen half of the combination fen/phen was withdrawn from the market.

_____ b. Connolly suspected that fen/phen was the cause of her patients' heart damage.

_____ c. The FDA conducted its own review of fen/phen.

4. Making Correct Inferences

Two of the statements below are correct *inferences*, or reasonable guesses. They are based on information in the passage. The other statement is an incorrect, or faulty, inference. Label the statements C for *correct* inference and F for *faulty* inference.

_____ a. Dr. Connolly's research helped take fen/phen off the market.

_____ b. Without Dr. Connolly's efforts, the danger of fen/phen would never have come to light.

_____ c. The drug combination fen/phen posed a real danger to the public.

5. Understanding Main Ideas

One of the statements below expresses the main idea of the passage. One statement is too general, or too broad. The other explains only part of the passage; it is too narrow. Label the statements M for *main idea*, B for *too broad*, and N for *too narrow*.

_____ a. Dr. Heidi Connolly is the doctor whose suspicions and research led to the rapid FDA recall of the drug fenfluramine.

_____ b. Connolly's patient had been taking a combination of drugs to lose weight.

_____ c. FDA approval of drugs may not guarantee the safety of those drugs.

Correct Answers, Part A _____

Correct Answers, Part B _____

Total Correct Answers _____

All the World Is a Stage

Acting is a momentary art; once the performance is over, there is nothing left but the memory of it. There is no history or record of acting itself before the end of the nineteenth century, but there are the written recollections of those people who saw it.

The great periods of acting are those in which actors were valued highly by society. Greek acting developed from the reciting and singing of poetic texts and from ritual dances honoring Dionysus, the god of wine and fertility. The first actor, tradition says, was Thespis, who introduced impersonation—pretending to be another person—to Athens in about 560 B.C. Early actors developed acting with a mask in order to portray several characters in one play. Through mime—stylized gestures indicating the characters' emotions—they made the body express what the face, hidden by a mask, could not.

The Romans derived their theater from that of the Greeks and further developed an emphasis on voice. The art of oratory, or public speaking, was often compared to acting, and the rules for orators have continued to influence actors. Actors in Rome were slaves, and the theater was viewed principally as entertainment. Acting as showmanship flourished as the virtuosity and beauty of an individual were emphasized.

Along with the serious acting tradition of the Greeks was a comical style of acting. Little is known about it except that it was very physical, relied on crude jokes and situations, and was apparently popular. Serious professional acting declined along with the Roman Empire and was suppressed by the church in the Middle Ages. Wandering minstrels kept the art of acting alive during this period.

In Elizabethan drama of the late sixteenth and early seventeenth centuries in England, actors faced the problem of portraying not types but individuals. The characters of Shakespeare demand that actors have an understanding of the psychology that is driving the action on stage. Still, Elizabethan acting was probably not acting in the modern sense. The emphasis was still on admirable vocal delivery and choice of gestures appropriate to the poet's words.

Superior acting has continued on the basis of strong national theatrical traditions; this is especially true in Great Britain. The popular theatrical traditions of minstrelsy, variety, and vaudeville culminated in the United States with a group of brilliant actors, including W. C. Fields and Will Rogers, whose work blossomed in early motion pictures.

Reading Time _____

Recalling Facts

1. In about 560 B.C., the Greek actor Thespis introduced
   - ❑ a. comedy.
   - ❑ b. impersonation.
   - ❑ c. mime.

2. Stylized gestures indicating the characters' emotions is called
   - ❑ a. impersonation.
   - ❑ b. oratory.
   - ❑ c. mime.

3. Often compared to acting, oratory is
   - ❑ a. ritual dancing.
   - ❑ b. reciting poetic texts.
   - ❑ c. public speaking.

4. During the Middle Ages, acting
   - ❑ a. flourished.
   - ❑ b. was suppressed.
   - ❑ c. was mostly comical.

5. W. C. Fields and Will Rogers became famous as
   - ❑ a. early motion picture actors.
   - ❑ b. minstrels.
   - ❑ c. orators.

Understanding Ideas

6. Orators, like actors,
   - ❑ a. place a great deal of emphasis on the voice.
   - ❑ b. pretend to be another person.
   - ❑ c. are entertainers.

7. You can conclude from the article that acting is
   - ❑ a. a modern invention.
   - ❑ b. a product of Western culture.
   - ❑ c. an ancient art form.

8. The aim of acting today is
   - ❑ a. largely ceremonial.
   - ❑ b. to entertain.
   - ❑ c. educational.

9. Elizabethan drama introduced a new element to acting, that is,
   - ❑ a. an understanding of the reasons behind actions on the stage.
   - ❑ b. gestures appropriate to the spoken word.
   - ❑ c. appropriate vocal interpretation.

10. During the long history of acting, actors have generally been considered
    - ❑ a. lowly entertainers.
    - ❑ b. important contributors to society.
    - ❑ c. politically influential.

Mark Stein is the stage manager for a production of *Guys and Dolls* at his university drama school. As stage manager, he has orchestrated the various parts of the production—stagehands and carpenters, properties and costumes, lighting, actors, and orchestra—making sure everyone does his or her job. Finally, the production is ready for opening night, but Mark's job does not end.

Mark gives the signal to dim the lights and raise the curtain, trying hard to start on time. Throughout the performance, he wears a head mike and calls cues for scenery changes, lighting, and everything that happens on stage. If a prop breaks or a zipper sticks during a costume change, that's his problem, and so Mark carries tape and safety pins and keeps his fingers crossed. During intermission, he makes sure that everything is ready for the second act, and he signals the house manager to dim the outside lights to call the audience back into the theater for the rest of the performance.

After curtain calls, Mark listens to complaints from everybody about things that didn't go right even if the audience didn't notice the problems. He writes everything down and promises to have it fixed by tomorrow. There are no curtain calls for stage managers, but plays wouldn't happen without them.

1. **Recognizing Words in Context**

Find the word *orchestrated* in the passage. One definition below is a *synonym* for that word; it means the same or almost the same thing. One definition is an *antonym*; it has the opposite or nearly opposite meaning. The other has a completely different meaning. Label the definitions S for *synonym*, A for *antonym*, and D for *different*.

_____ a. disarranged

_____ b. coordinated

_____ c. enjoyed

2. **Distinguishing Fact from Opinion**

Two of the statements below present *facts*, which can be proved correct. The other statement is an *opinion*, which expresses someone's thoughts or beliefs. Label the statements F for *fact* and O for *opinion*.

_____ a. Mark makes sure everyone does his or her job.

_____ b. Mark wears a head mike and calls cues during the performance.

_____ c. Plays wouldn't happen without stage managers.

3. Keeping Events in Order

Label the statements below 1, 2, and 3 to show the order in which the events happened.

_____ a. Mark listens to everyone's complaints after the first performance.

_____ b. Mark calls the cues for scenery changes.

_____ c. Mark coordinates the parts of the production during rehearsals.

4. Making Correct Inferences

Two of the statements below are correct *inferences*, or reasonable guesses. They are based on information in the passage. The other statement is an incorrect, or faulty, inference. Label the statements C for *correct* inference and F for *faulty* inference.

_____ a. The stage manager's job requires a good head for details.

_____ b. Stage managers have little to do during theatrical productions.

_____ c. A stage manager should not expect praise and recognition.

5. Understanding Main Ideas

One of the statements below expresses the main idea of the passage. One statement is too general, or too broad. The other explains only part of the passage; it is too narrow. Label the statements M for *main idea*, B for *too broad*, and N for *too narrow*.

_____ a. One backstage job is that of stage manager.

_____ b. If a prop breaks or a zipper sticks during a production, it is the stage manager's problem.

_____ c. The stage manager coordinates a theatrical production, solves problems, and keeps the show running.

Correct Answers, Part A _____

Correct Answers, Part B _____

Governments support themselves by taking a portion of the wealth of their citizens mainly through taxation, but governments also have other ways of raising money. State governments, for example, sell license plates for automobiles, and they charge fees for licensing drivers. Local governments sell operating licenses to owners of businesses as well as charge fees for marriage licenses, pet licenses, vehicle stickers, and parking cars.

One of the ways in which many governments raise money is through lotteries. Lotteries have proven to be an effective means for governments, churches, fraternal societies, and other organizations to raise money. A lottery is a form of gambling in which people buy chances, called lottery tickets, in the hope of winning one or more prizes. Prizes offered by organizations may be goods such as automobiles, television sets, and other appliances; or they may be money prizes.

What differentiates a lottery from a tax is that no one is forced to take part. Wherever lotteries are offered, however, they have proved quite popular. In many places, the money raised is used for specific purposes such as funding education or public projects. Government lotteries or large-scale private ones are found in many African and Middle East states, most European countries, Latin American nations, Japan, and Australia. In North America, Canada has a national lottery, but the United States does not have a national lottery although a number of states maintain lotteries. In the 1960s, New Hampshire, New York, and New Jersey were the first states to adopt lotteries as a means of raising funds. Many other states have since established lotteries.

In some lotteries, particularly in Europe, where the prizes may be very large, ticket prices are also very high. It is possible, however, to buy fractions of a ticket. Winners, of course, receive only a fraction of a large prize if they have bought less than a whole ticket.

Because of the very large number of people who buy lottery tickets, promoters now use computers to issue tickets and to keep track of the numbers sold. By computer, it is also possible to determine how many winning tickets have been sold after a drawing has taken place. In the United States, opponents to state lotteries have criticized lotteries saying that many who play are those who can least afford it, and even though people play by free choice, lotteries amount to a regressive tax.

Reading Time _____

Recalling Facts

1. A lottery is a form of
   - ❏ a. taxation.
   - ❏ b. gambling.
   - ❏ c. licensing.

2. What differentiates a lottery from a tax is that
   - ❏ a. it is run by the government.
   - ❏ b. the money gained is used for specific purposes.
   - ❏ c. no one is forced to take part.

3. People buy lottery tickets in order to
   - ❏ a. win prizes.
   - ❏ b. make charitable donations.
   - ❏ c. oppose taxes.

4. Winners of the main lottery prize usually receive
   - ❏ a. free lottery tickets.
   - ❏ b. free education.
   - ❏ c. goods or money.

5. In North America, a country with a national lottery is
   - ❏ a. the United States.
   - ❏ b. New Jersey.
   - ❏ c. Canada.

Understanding Ideas

6. It is likely that lotteries are popular because
   - ❏ a. many people like to gamble.
   - ❏ b. the money raised is used for good causes.
   - ❏ c. everybody wins.

7. Fees for licenses are similar to taxes because
   - ❏ a. prizes are awarded.
   - ❏ b. there is no free choice.
   - ❏ c. private businesses are exempt.

8. Before the use of computers for lotteries,
   - ❏ a. few people bought lottery tickets.
   - ❏ b. it was difficult to run large lotteries efficiently.
   - ❏ c. lotteries were smaller in size.

9. You can conclude from the article that lotteries are
   - ❏ a. a successful method for governments to earn money.
   - ❏ b. not an effective means for raising funds.
   - ❏ c. more successful if run on a national rather than on a state level.

10. Using lotteries to raise public funds is an idea that is
    - ❏ a. universally popular.
    - ❏ b. doomed to fail.
    - ❏ c. controversial.

"Dad, it's allowance time!" Nick announced cheerfully, holding out his hand for his weekly allowance.

Nick's father looked embarrassed as he apologized. "Sorry, Nick, I'm a little short this week, but your mother can pay your allowance."

Nick asked his mother for his allowance, and said. "This is the second week that Dad told me to ask you for my allowance. Why is Dad so strapped for cash lately?"

"Why don't you ask Dad to explain it to you?" his mother replied with a frown.

Nick went back into the living room where his father had just turned on the television. "Dad, Mom said I should ask you why there's a problem with money this week—and last week, too."

"Wait a minute, Nick," his father said. His father watched the TV screen intently as table tennis balls bounced out of a cage, and a young woman announced the number on each ball. In front of Nick's father was a pile of lottery tickets that he ripped up, exclaiming "Lost again!" Then he looked up at Nick and said, "This week's jackpot was 11 million dollars, Nick! Do you know what we could do with 11 million dollars?"

Now Nick knew that his allowance had probably been spent on losing lottery tickets.

1. Recognizing Words in Context

Find the word *short* in the passage. One definition below is a *synonym* for that word; it means the same or almost the same thing. One definition is an *antonym;* it has the opposite or nearly opposite meaning. The other has a completely different meaning. Label the definitions S for *synonym,* A for *antonym,* and D for *different.*

_____ a. not tall

_____ b. lacking

_____ c. plentiful

2. Distinguishing Fact from Opinion

Two of the statements below present *facts,* which can be proved correct. The other statement is an *opinion,* which expresses someone's thoughts or beliefs. Label the statements F for *fact* and O for *opinion.*

_____ a. Nick's father could not give Nick his allowance.

_____ b. Nick's father was foolish to have spent so much money on lottery tickets.

_____ c. The lottery jackpot was 11 million dollars.

3. Keeping Events in Order

Label the statements below 1, 2, and 3 to show the order in which the events happened.

_____ a. Nick asked his father for his allowance.

_____ b. A woman announced the numbers on the table tennis balls.

_____ c. Nick's father tore up his lottery tickets.

4. Making Correct Inferences

Two of the statements below are correct *inferences*, or reasonable guesses. They are based on information in the passage. The other statement is an incorrect, or faulty, inference. Label the statements C for *correct* inference and F for *faulty* inference.

_____ a. Nick's father had no money because he had spent it all on lottery tickets.

_____ b. Nick and his mother were upset that money was being wasted on lottery tickets.

_____ c. Nick wanted his allowance so that he could buy lottery tickets too.

5. Understanding Main Ideas

One of the statements below expresses the main idea of the passage. One statement is too general, or too broad. The other explains only part of the passage; it is too narrow. Label the statements M for *main idea*, B for *too broad*, and N for *too narrow*.

_____ a. A lottery is a form of gambling in which people buy chances in hopes of winning prizes.

_____ b. Nick's father has been spending a lot of money on lottery tickets in hopes of winning a big jackpot.

_____ c. Nick's father did not have enough money to give Nick his allowance.

Correct Answers, Part A _____

Correct Answers, Part B _____

Total Correct Answers _____

Fermentation is a chemical change in animal and vegetable matter brought about by microscopic yeasts, bacteria, and molds. Examples of fermentation are the souring of milk, the rising of bread dough, and the conversion of sugars and starches to alcohol. Many industrial chemicals and a number of antibiotics used in modern medicine are produced by fermentation under controlled conditions.

The result of fermentation is usually that a substance is broken down into simpler compounds. In some cases, fermentation is used to change a material in a way that would be difficult or very costly if ordinary chemical methods were chosen. Fermentation is always initiated by enzymes formed in the cells of living organisms. An enzyme is a natural catalyst that brings about a chemical change without being affected itself.

The products of fermentation have been used since earliest times. Cave dwellers discovered that aged meat has a more pleasing flavor than the meat of freshly killed game. Wine, beer, and leavened bread are as old as agriculture; and cheese, which involves the fermentation of milk or cream, is another ancient food. The medicinal value of fermented products has been known for a long time. The Chinese used moldy soybean curd to cure skin infections 3,000 years ago, and the early Central American Indians treated infected wounds with fungi.

Fermentation chemistry is a new science that is still in its earliest stages. It is the basis of manufacturing processes that convert raw materials such as grains, sugars, and industrial by-products into many different synthetic products. Carefully selected strains of yeasts, bacteria, and molds are used. Penicillin is an antibiotic that destroys many disease-causing bacteria. It is derived from a mold that grows in a fermenting mixture of substances, which were carefully selected for this purpose. The manufacture of penicillin and many other antibiotics has become an important branch of the drug industry.

Citric acid is one of many chemicals produced by microorganisms. It is used in metal cleaners and as a preservative and flavoring agent in foods. Citric acid, which is responsible for the tartness of citrus fruits, could be obtained from the fruit, but it would take thousands of trees to produce the amount of citric acid made by the fermentation of molasses with a special mold. Certain vitamins are made by mold fermentation; and enzymes themselves, extracted from various microorganisms, have many uses in the manufacture of foods and drugs.

Reading Time _____

Recalling Facts

1. Fermentation is a
   - ❏ a. kind of bacteria.
   - ❏ b. chemical change.
   - ❏ c. synthetic product.

2. Fermentation is always initiated by
   - ❏ a. molds.
   - ❏ b. bacteria.
   - ❏ c. enzymes.

3. Fermentation occurs
   - ❏ a. wherever bacteria are present.
   - ❏ b. in animal and vegetable matter.
   - ❏ c. primarily in liquid substances.

4. Citric acid can be made by fermenting
   - ❏ a. molasses.
   - ❏ b. milk.
   - ❏ c. grains.

5. A product of fermentation used by cave dwellers was
   - ❏ a. cheese.
   - ❏ b. antibiotics.
   - ❏ c. aged meat.

Understanding Ideas

6. You can conclude from the article that when fermentation takes place,
   - ❏ a. the substance that is fermented undergoes a change.
   - ❏ b. the resulting substance is more useful than the initial substance.
   - ❏ c. there is no change in the original substance.

7. The earliest uses of fermentation probably resulted from
   - ❏ a. accidental discoveries.
   - ❏ b. extensive testing.
   - ❏ c. the need to save money.

8. It is likely that the usefulness of fermentation chemistry
   - ❏ a. has run its course.
   - ❏ b. will expand greatly.
   - ❏ c. is yet to be appreciated by scientists.

9. Experiments with fermentation involve
   - ❏ a. measuring how high bread rises.
   - ❏ b. testing how different enzymes react with various substances.
   - ❏ c. determining chemical changes in enzymes.

10. The fermentation process is useful
    - ❏ a. mainly in medical research.
    - ❏ b. in a wide variety of industries.
    - ❏ c. mainly in the food industry.

Marta stood beneath a towering saguaro cactus, using a long pole to knock off the ripe saguaro fruit. Other Papago women and children picked up the fallen fruit, split it open, scooped out the pulp and black seeds, and put them in a basket. Then the women and children carefully placed the open red husks of the fruit on the ground around the cactus to help bring the summer rains.

When the basket was full, the women and children returned to their temporary camp among the groves of cacti. One of the first things they did with the fruit was make saguaro syrup. Each family donated some syrup to make saguaro wine for the nawait ceremony, which was held to bring the life-giving summer rains to their Sonoran Desert home.

The syrup was first ritually cleansed by a shaman, or priest, and then the men began the process of fermenting it inside a round grass house. Outside the fermentation house, ceremonies took place with speeches, singing, and dancing. When the wine was ready, all the people gathered for the "sit and drink" ceremony. Cup bearers served wine to everyone while speeches were made and the chief rain shaman sang. As Marta sipped her wine, she looked hopefully up at the sky for the first sign of clouds.

1. Recognizing Words in Context

Find the word *gathered* in the passage. One definition below is a *synonym* for that word; it means the same or almost the same thing. One definition is an *antonym*; it has the opposite or nearly opposite meaning. The other has a completely different meaning. Label the definitions S for *synonym*, A for *antonym*, and D for *different*.

_____ a. separated

_____ b. harvested

_____ c. assembled

2. Distinguishing Fact from Opinion

Two of the statements below present *facts*, which can be proved correct. The other statement is an *opinion*, which expresses someone's thoughts or beliefs. Label the statements F for *fact* and O for *opinion*.

_____ a. Drinking saguaro wine during the nawait ceremony would bring the summer rains.

_____ b. Women and children gathered the saguaro fruit.

_____ c. Men fermented the saguaro syrup until it became wine.

3. Keeping Events in Order

Two of the statements below describe events that happened at the same time. The other statement describes an event that happened before or after those events. Label them S for *same time*, B for *before*, and A for *after*.

_____ a. The wine was being fermented inside a grass house.

_____ b. Ceremonies were held with speeches, singing, and dancing.

_____ c. A shaman ritually cleansed the saguaro syrup.

4. Making Correct Inferences

Two of the statements below are correct *inferences*, or reasonable guesses. They are based on information in the passage. The other statement is an incorrect, or faulty, inference. Label the statements C for *correct* inference and F for *faulty* inference.

_____ a. The Papago were not aware of the natural events that brought the summer rains.

_____ b. The coming of the summer rains was especially important to the Papago.

_____ c. The Papago believed that the nawait ceremony would cause the rains to come.

5. Understanding Main Ideas

One of the statements below expresses the main idea of the passage. One statement is too general, or too broad. The other explains only part of the passage; it is too narrow. Label the statements M for *main idea*, B for *too broad*, and N for *too narrow*.

_____ a. Every Papago family donated saguaro syrup for the nawait ceremony.

_____ b. The Sonoran Desert of southwestern Arizona has long been home to the Papago people.

_____ c. The Papago people hold a ceremony each year to bring the summer rains.

Correct Answers, Part A _____

Correct Answers, Part B _____

Total Correct Answers _____

Answer Key

Reading Rate Graph

Comprehension Score Graph

Comprehension Skills Profile Graph

ANSWER KEY

1A	1. a	2. a	3. b	4. b	5. a	6. b	7. c	8. b	9. c	10. a
1B	1. D, S, A	2. F, O, F	3. 1, 2, 3	4. C, C, F	5. N, B, M					
2A	1. b	2. b	3. b	4. c	5. c	6. a	7. a	8. c	9. c	10. b
2B	1. A, S, D	2. F, F, O	3. 2, 3, 1	4. C, F, C	5. B, N, M					
3A	1. b	2. a	3. c	4. c	5. a	6. a	7. c	8. a	9. b	10. a
3B	1. S, A, D	2. F, F, O	3. S, S, A	4. F, C, C	5. M, N, B					
4A	1. c	2. b	3. a	4. b	5. a	6. b	7. c	8. b	9. b	10. c
4B	1. S, A, D	2. F, F, O	3. 1, 3, 2	4. F, C, C	5. M, N, B					
5A	1. a	2. c	3. c	4. b	5. b	6. b	7. c	8. a	9. b	10. c
5B	1. S, D, A	2. F, O, F	3. 2, 1, 3	4. C, F, C	5. B, M, N					
6A	1. c	2. b	3. c	4. c	5. a	6. c	7. b	8. a	9. a	10. b
6B	1. D, A, S	2. O, F, F	3. S, S, A	4. C, F, C	5. M, B, N					
7A	1. b	2. b	3. c	4. a	5. a	6. a	7. a	8. b	9. c	10. b
7B	1. S, D, A	2. F, O, F	3. 1, 3, 2	4. C, C, F	5. N, M, B					
8A	1. c	2. c	3. b	4. b	5. b	6. a	7. b	8. b	9. a	10. c
8B	1. S, A, D	2. F, O, F	3. 1, 3, 2	4. C, F, C	5. B, N, M					
9A	1. c	2. a	3. b	4. c	5. c	6. b	7. c	8. c	9. b	10. a
9B	1. A, D, S	2. O, F, F	3. S, A, S	4. C, F, C	5. N, M, B					
10A	1. b	2. a	3. b	4. b	5. a	6. c	7. c	8. a	9. b	10. a
10B	1. A, S, D	2. O, F, F	3. 3, 2, 1	4. C, C, F	5. M, B, N					
11A	1. c	2. a	3. a	4. b	5. a	6. c	7. b	8. b	9. b	10. a
11B	1. A, S, D	2. O, F, F	3. A, S, S	4. C, F, C	5. B, N, M					
12A	1. a	2. a	3. b	4. c	5. a	6. b	7. c	8. a	9. b	10. c
12B	1. A, S, D	2. O, F, F	3. 1, 2, 3	4. C, C, F	5. N, M, B					
13A	1. a	2. b	3. c	4. a	5. b	6. b	7. c	8. a	9. a	10. b
13B	1. D, A, S	2. F, O, F	3. 2, 3, 1	4. F, C, C	5. B, N, M					

14A	1. c	2. a	3. a	4. c	5. b	6. b	7. a	8. b	9. c	10. c
14B	1. A, S, D		2. F, F, O		3. 2, 3, 1		4. F, C, C		5. B, N, M	
15A	1. b	2. a	3. b	4. c	5. b	6. a	7. a	8. b	9. c	10. a
15B	1. A, S, D		2. O, F, F		3. 1, 2, 3		4. C, F, C		5. B, N, M	
16A	1. a	2. c	3. b	4. c	5. b	6. a	7. c	8. a	9. b	10. c
16B	1. D, A, S		2. F, F, O		3. A, S, S		4. C, F, C		5. M, B, N	
17A	1. a	2. c	3. b	4. a	5. c	6. a	7. b	8. b	9. c	10. b
17B	1. A, D, S		2. F, O, F		3. S, A, S		4. C, F, C		5. B, N, M	
18A	1. c	2. a	3. c	4. b	5. b	6. c	7. b	8. b	9. c	10. a
18B	1. S, A, D		2. O, F, F		3. S, B, S		4. C, F, C		5. N, M, B	
19A	1. c	2. b	3. a	4. b	5. b	6. a	7. b	8. b	9. c	10. c
19B	1. A, D, S		2. F, F, O		3. 2, 1, 3		4. C, F, C		5. N, B, M	
20A	1. c	2. c	3. b	4. c	5. a	6. a	7. a	8. b	9. b	10. a
20B	1. D, S, A		2. F, F, O		3. 3, 1, 2		4. C, F, C		5. B, M, N	
21A	1. c	2. a	3. b	4. c	5. a	6. b	7. c	8. a	9. a	10. a
21B	1. S, A, D		2. F, O, F		3. B, S, S		4. F, C, C		5. N, M, B	
22A	1. c	2. c	3. a	4. a	5. c	6. b	7. b	8. b	9. a	10. a
22B	1. D, S, A		2. F, O, F		3. 3, 1, 2		4. C, F, C		5. M, N, B	
23A	1. b	2. c	3. c	4. b	5. a	6. a	7. c	8. b	9. a	10. b
23B	1. A, S, D		2. F, F, O		3. 3, 2, 1		4. C, F, C		5. B, N, M	
24A	1. b	2. c	3. a	4. c	5. c	6. a	7. b	8. b	9. a	10. a
24B	1. A, S, D		2. F, O, F		3. 1, 2, 3		4. C, C, F		5. B, M, N	
25A	1. b	2. c	3. b	4. a	5. c	6. a	7. a	8. b	9. b	10. b
25B	1. A, D, S		2. O, F, F		3. S, S, B		4. F, C, C		5. N, B, M	

READING RATE

Put an X on the line above each lesson number to show your reading time and words-per-minute rate for that unit.

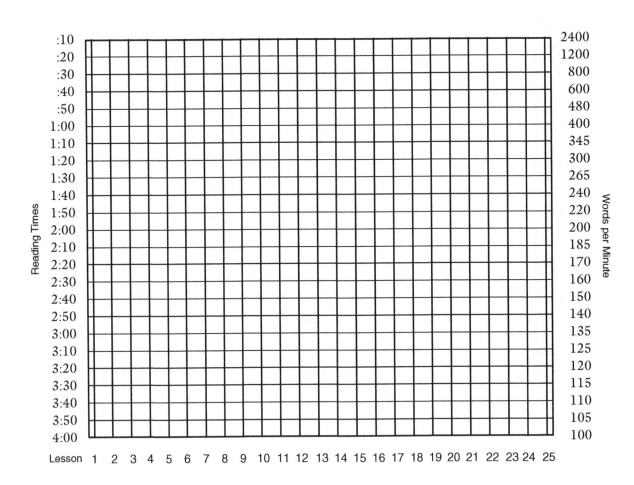

COMPREHENSION SCORE

Put an X on the line above each lesson number to indicate your total correct answers and comprehension score for that unit.

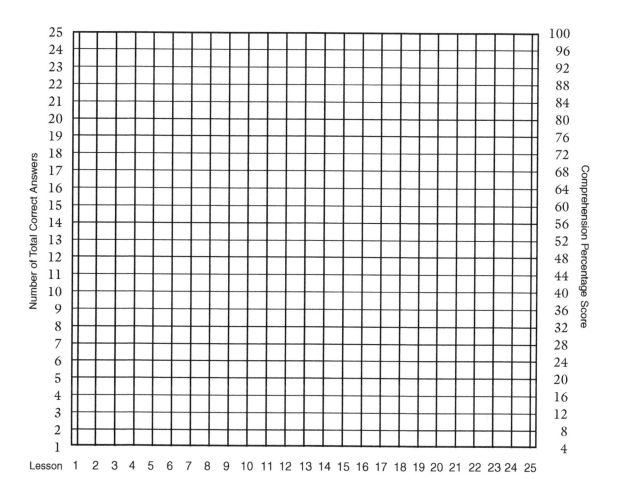

COMPREHENSION SKILLS PROFILE

Put an X in the box above each question type to indicate an incorrect reponse to any part of that question.

	Recognizing Words in Context	Distinguishing Fact from Opinion	Keeping Events in Order	Making Correct Inferences	Understanding Main Ideas
Lesson 1					
2					
3					
4					
5					
6					
7					
8					
9					
10					
11					
12					
13					
14					
15					
16					
17					
18					
19					
20					
21					
22					
23					
24					
25					